Healthy Grilling

Healthy Grilling

Sizzling Favorites for Indoor and Outdoor Grills

Barbara Grunes

Longmont, Colorado

Snowcap Press
PO Box 123
Longmont, Colorado 80502-0123
http://www.snowcappress.com; info@snowcappress.com

ISBN: 0-9669701-3-6

Library of Congress Card Number: 00-106970

Printed in the United States of America

On the cover: Chicken With Nectarines and Raspberries
Digital imagery © 2001 PhotoDisc, Inc.

Contents

Introduction

Everyone loves food cooked on the grill, whether it's meat, poultry, fish, vegetables, or fruit. Thanks to indoor electric countertop grills and outdoor gas grills, grilling is now a year-round activity. You can bring that "taste of summer" into your home anytime you like, June or January.

Grilling is a casual mode of cooking that goes so well with festive occasions. In fact, with an electric tabletop grill, you can arrange a variety of meats, fish, or vegetables on a tray and let guests grill the food themselves—fun for them and a time-saver for you.

Grilling is also an excellent way to cook foods with little fat but plenty of flavor, an important consideration in these times of heightened awareness regarding health concerns. One of my intentions in writing this cookbook has been to demonstrate the strong health advantage to this clever alternative to frying, and encourage you to grill not only the standards such as chicken breast and hamburgers, but fruits, vegetables, and grains that you may not even have thought of grilling before. The new tabletop grills cook foods quickly, retaining nutritional value, have ridged surfaces that allow fat to drip away, and create little or no smoke.

Because it's such a quick and convenient cooking method, grilling may encourage you to eat a greater variety of healthy foods. The countertop grills, especially, make preparation and cleanup simple; they're no more complicated than an electric skillet. Just plug them in and preheat. After cooking, let the grill cool, then simply wash all the pieces with soapy sponge and wipe dry. Some parts of most machines are submersible, or even dishwasher safe. Be sure to check the manufacturer's directions.

When shopping for an indoor grill, your first choice is whether to buy a contact grill or a regular flat grill. Contact grills have two cooking surfaces that are hinged together, like a waffle iron. Both sides of the food grill at once. Contact grills cook foods very quickly, and you don't have to turn most foods, making them very convenient. They tend to be more expensive than flat grills. And you cannot grill very soft foods such as cherry tomatoes or bulky foods such as corn on the cob on many contact grills. Some brands of contact grills do flip open if you need to cook on a flat surface.

Many, but not all, grills come with adjustable thermostats. Always start cooking over medium-high to high heat. This technique sears the food, then you can lower the heat to finish the cooking.

Many grills have grease pans or channels, which let fats drain away and cut down on smoke. Some have a water basin that sits underneath the grilling surface, which cuts down on smoke. Besides water, you can add other liquids, such as apple cider, to the basin to moisten and flavor foods. You can even add garlic, herbs or spices, orange or lemon slices, or a bit of smoke flavoring to the basin to infuse foods with extra flavor.

Indoor grills are small enough to set right on the countertop. It is a good idea to use the grill near an open window or other ventilation. Although some grills are virtually smoke-free, others do create some smoke.

Other features you may want to look for, depending on your needs, are grease pans, non-exposed heating elements, splatter guards, handles that stay cool, larger cooking surfaces, higher wattage (for faster cooking), and nonstick cooking grids. Some grills have skewers and skewer racks.

For an outdoor grill, you'll want gas or charcoal. Gas grills are increasingly popular because they offer more convenience than charcoal grills. At a minimum, you'll probably want a grill with at least two burners (with individual heat controls), a sturdy cart, a grease catcher, and burners and grids made of high-quality materials. Paying more will get you such features as extra grill burners, a wider range of temperature controls, side burners, and a bigger cooking grid.

Although I emphasize electric grills and gas grills because they're so popular, there's absolutely no reason you can't make any of these recipes on a charcoal grill or in a stovetop grill pan. The cooking times may vary.

General food preparation and grilling tips

• Although preparing ingredients from scratch is the best way to preserve their flavors, a busy cook is easily tempted by the wide variety of packaged foods in the supermarket. To save time, take advantage of washed and mixed salad greens, cored fresh pineapple, trimmed and chopped vegetables, peeled and minced garlic and ginger, peeled potatoes, fresh herbs, ready-made polenta, and bottled salsas, dressings, and pasta sauces.

• Use freezer-weight plastic bags for marinating meats. To save time, put the marinade ingredients directly in the bag, and stir them right in the bag. Be sure to seal bags tightly. To be on the safe side, you can put the bag in a bowl in case it leaks.

• Always preheat the grill, using the manufacturer's directions as a guide. Usually this takes only a few minutes.

• Use nonstick cooking sprays to oil grill surfaces and foods. They add only the tiniest amount of fat while helping foods to brown beautifully. These sprays come in a variety of flavors, including olive oil, butter, garlic, and lemon. Note that in some recipes, I call for both the food and the cooking surface to be sprayed. This may make foods slide on nonstick grills that are on a slant. If you find that foods are sliding too much, very lightly spray either the food or the grill, but not both.

• Choose healthful oils high in monounsaturated fats, such as olive oil and canola oil or canola-corn oil blend. Extra virgin olive oil has a lovely, intense flavor and is good for flavoring dressings and marinades or for drizzling over cooked foods. It's expensive to use for oiling the grilling surface. Use regular olive oil or a cooking spray for that purpose. Don't worry about the amount of oil in marinades. Much of it is not absorbed by the food. Note that if you keep oils in the refrigerator, they may turn cloudy. They will clear up once they come to room temperature.

• Use low-sodium soy sauce if you are trying to limit your salt intake.

• Most recipe instructions say "turn as needed." Generally, you will need to turn foods at least once if you're cooking on a flat-surface countertop or outdoor grill. If you are cooking on a contact grill, you often do not need to turn the food at all.

• To make the recipes suitable for smaller indoor grills, I give the instructions in steps—for example, grill the meat, then the vegetable that accompanies it. If you're using a larger grill, you may be able to grill the foods side by side.

• I call for light beer in some of the marinades. While you can use a reduced-calorie beer, "light" refers to the color. Use a pilsner (lager) or ale in marinades. A stout or other strongly flavored beer will overpower the food.

• Refrigerate leftover grilled foods and use in salads, soups, and other dishes. Or, freeze them for up to a month. Reheat in the microwave.

• Nearly all of these dishes are low to moderate in fat content and fit nicely into a healthful diet. To keep saturated fat to a minimum, I use lean poultry and meats, low-fat or nonfat dairy products, and plenty of fruits and vegetables. When recipes do contain a fair amount of fat, it is usually in the form of "healthier" fats such as olive or canola oil, or fish oils. Occasionally I use a small amount of butter or margarine when the flavor of a dish really requires it.

Important!

Grilling is not an exact science. Cooking times depend on the thickness of the food, the type of grill and how hot it gets, and how often you turn the food. The range of times given in each recipe applies to countertop electric grills. (The shorter time will be for smaller pieces of food on contact grills; the longer time for thicker pieces of food and/or cooking on lower-watt flat grills.) In each recipe, I also provide a time range for cooking over medium heat on an outdoor gas grill. Don't rely solely on cooking times, however, or even the grill's automatic shutoff. Judge doneness by how the food looks and feels, and for meat or poultry, by whether the juices run clear when you cut into it.

Meat and Poultry

It's hard to resist the smell of grilling meat and poultry.

Unfortunately, so many of the meats we love to grill—hamburgers, hot dogs, ribs, steaks, chicken wings—tend to be loaded with fat and saturated fat. Fortunately, leaner alternatives to all these meats are easy to find. Even sausage has slimmed down. Many supermarkets now carry lower-fat alternatives such as chicken sausage, flavored with apple, basil, or other appealing "extras."

I devote much of this chapter to recipes for chicken breast. That's no accident. Chicken breast is one of the most popular choices for healthy eating. High in protein, low in fat and calories, relatively inexpensive, and conveniently packaged, chicken breast also is versatile. You can dress it up with just about anything, from the pungency of garlic to the smoky caramel of grilled fruit.

Turkey breast, once a treat for Thanksgiving tables, is now readily available year-round. It is even leaner than chicken, and has its own distinct, delicate flavor. It can become very dry if overcooked, so watch it carefully on the grill.

Turkey and chicken can be used interchangeably in many of these recipes, though the cooking time may need to be adjusted up or down a bit. Recipes with pork often taste good made with chicken instead, and vice versa.

Leaner meats do require a bit more care. They often benefit from a bath in marinade, and it's important not to overcook them.

I give a range of cooking times in recipes, mostly for indoor grills. The shortest cooking times would be for contact grills. Plan on slightly longer cooking times on an outdoor gas or charcoal grill. Because meats vary in thickness and grills vary in hotness, don't rely solely on cooking times to tell when a meat is done.

Buying, preparing, and grilling meat and poultry

• Choose lean cuts. Trim all the visible fat from meats, and remove the skin from poultry. (You can cook poultry with the skin to retain some juiciness, then remove the skin after cooking.) Some lean choices include turkey breast, bison (buffalo), chicken breast, pork tenderloin and center loin, beef round (top, tip, and eye), beef top loin and top sirloin, and lamb sirloin.

• To make it easier to slice meat into thin strips, freeze it until the meat is firm but can still be pierced with a fork.

• To avoid stringiness, always slice meats and poultry against the grain.

• Keep meats and poultry chilled until it's time to grill them, and always thaw frozen meats and poultry in the refrigerator. Bacteria can multiply quickly at room temperature. If you're short on time, you can thaw meats and poultry, still in their wrappings, in a sinkful of cold water. Allow 1 hour per pound, and refresh the water every 30 minutes so it stays cold.

• Go light on the salt before grilling as it draws out juices.

• Do not overcook lean meats as they become tough.

• Foods continue to cook after you remove them from the heat, so let meat or poultry rest a couple of minutes after cooking before you serve it. This gives you time to grill accompaniments such as fruits or vegetables.

• You can judge the doneness of meats and poultry by cutting into them, or by using a thermometer. Non-ground cuts of lamb and beef should be cooked to at least 145 degrees F (medium rare). Pork should be cooked to 160 degrees. White-meat poultry needs to cook to 170 degrees, or until it no longer has traces of pink (although a little redness right near the bone is OK). Dark-meat poultry should cook to 180 degrees.

Always cook ground meats all the way through so there's no pink in the center (160 degrees), especially if you're going to serve them to children. Grinding meat distributes surface bacteria such as Salmonella and E. coli throughout the meat. Some of these bacteria can pose serious health risks, especially to children.

• When you're grilling plain chicken breasts, you can grill them with the skin on. The skin helps keep the chicken moist and adds very little fat, as long as you remove it after grilling.

• When cooking ground meat patties, it can be difficult to get the middle cooked through before the outsides turn to sawdust. Here's a helpful tip we gleaned from the August 2000 issue of Cook's Illustrated magazine: make the outsides of the patty thicker than the center. Use your thumbs to make an indentation in the center of the burger, so the middle is thinner than the outsides of the patty. As the burger cooks and shrinks toward the center, it will even out in thickness.

• I recommend cooking sausages through even when the package instructions don't say to. Otherwise, you may end up having to incinerate them on the grill to get the center cooked through.

Chicken With Nectarines and Raspberries

Makes 4 servings

1 cup fresh or prepared lime juice
2 teaspoons Jamaican jerk seasoning (optional)
½ cup coarsely chopped fresh cilantro
1 pound boneless, skinless chicken breasts (4 pieces)
Olive oil-flavored nonstick cooking spray
Salt and pepper
4 ripe nectarines, washed and sliced
1 cup fresh raspberries, washed and drained
2 limes, sliced, for garnish

Pour lime juice, seasoning, and cilantro into a large, self-sealing plastic bag. Add chicken pieces and seal securely. Turn bag several times so that all of the chicken is touched by marinade. Refrigerate and marinate the chicken for 3 to 4 hours. Drain.

Preheat grill according to manufacturer's directions. Spray chicken breasts and grill, turning as needed, for 3 to 8 minutes, or until chicken is slightly firm to the touch and juices run clear when it is pierced with a knife. Season with salt and pepper.

Spray nectarine slices and grill a minute or two, turning as needed, until warmed through. Toss cooked nectarines with raspberries.

Serve chicken with nectarine slices and raspberries. Garnish with sliced lime.

Outdoor grill: 12 to 14 minutes for chicken, 2 to 3 minutes for nectarines

Chicken Breasts With Portobello Mushrooms

Makes 4 servings

⅓ cup extra virgin olive oil
¼ cup freshly squeezed lemon juice
1 teaspoon dried sage or 2 teaspoons fresh minced sage,
  divided
1 teaspoon prepared mustard
2 bay leaves
1 pound boneless, skinless chicken breasts (4 pieces)
4 large portobello mushrooms, cleaned and stems
  removed
Olive oil-flavored cooking spray
Salt and pepper

To make marinade: Combine oil, lemon juice, ½ teaspoon dried or 1 teaspoon fresh sage, mustard, and bay leaves. Pour marinade into self-sealing plastic bag. Add chicken breasts and seal bag securely closed. Turn bag a few times so that all portions of chicken are coated by marinade. Refrigerate and marinate for 1 to 2 hours. Drain, discarding marinade.

Preheat grill according to manufacturer's directions. Cook chicken for 3 to 8 minutes, turning as needed, or until chicken is slightly firm to the touch and juices run clear when chicken is pierced with a knife. Remove chicken to serving dish and keep warm.

Spray mushrooms and grilling surface with cooking spray. Place mushrooms on grill and sprinkle with ½ teaspoon dried sage or 1 teaspoon fresh. Grill 8 to 12 minutes, turning as needed, or until cooked through but still firm. Remove to serving dish. Season chicken and mushrooms with salt and pepper.

Outdoor grill: 12 to 14 minutes for chicken, 10 to 15 minutes for mushrooms

Chicken With Grilled Fresh Plums

Makes 4 servings

4 to 6 fresh plums, washed, pitted, and cut in half
  lengthwise
2 teaspoons minced ginger
2 teaspoons sugar mixed with ½ teaspoon ground cinnamon
Butter-flavored cooking spray
1 pound boneless, skinless chicken breasts, in 4 pieces
Salt and pepper to taste

Set plums on a plate, cut sides up, and sprinkle with ginger and cinnamon sugar. Set aside.

Preheat grill according to manufacturer's directions. Spray grilling surface with cooking spray. Spray chicken with cooking spray. Grill for 3 to 8 minutes, turning as needed, or until juices run clear when chicken is pierced with a knife.

Set chicken on serving plate. Sprinkle with salt and pepper. Spray grilling surface with cooking spray. Grill plums for 2 to 4 minutes, turning as needed, or until tender and lightly browned. Arrange plums over chicken and serve.

Outdoor grill: 12 to 14 minutes for chicken, 4 to 6 minutes for plums

Asian-Style Chicken With Black Beans

Makes 4 servings

1 tablespoon Asian fermented black beans (see note)
1 tablespoon canola blend oil
2 teaspoons minced garlic
3 green onions, chopped
½ cup chicken broth
3 tablespoons dry white wine
2 teaspoons soy sauce
1 teaspoon sugar
2 teaspoons cornstarch
1 pound boneless, skinless chicken breasts, cut into
   1-inch strips
Cooking spray

Prepare the sauce: Rinse black beans in a small strainer; drain. Mash beans with back of a spoon. Heat oil in a wok or a saucepan. Fry beans, garlic, and green onions.

In a saucepan, mix chicken broth, wine, soy sauce, and sugar. Remove 1 tablespoon of sauce and mix with the cornstarch. Mix cornstarch mixture into sauce. Add to black bean mixture in saucepan. Simmer until sauce thickens slightly, stirring occasionally. Remove sauce from heat and set aside.

Preheat grill according to manufacturer's directions. Spray grilling surface with cooking spray. Brush chicken breasts with sauce. Cook chicken 2 to 5 minutes, turning as needed, until it is slightly firm to the touch and juices run clear when it is pierced with a knife. Remove chicken pieces to individual plates. Drizzle with reheated sauce. Serve chicken hot, with rice.

Outdoor grill: 8 to 10 minutes

Note: Black beans, which are fermented, salted soybeans, are available in Asian groceries and some supermarkets.

Lemon Chicken With Potatoes

Makes 4 servings

½ cup freshly squeezed lemon juice
3 teaspoons minced garlic, divided
¼ teaspoon salt
⅛ teaspoon white pepper
3 teaspoons dried basil, divided
2 teaspoons dried, crushed rosemary
4 large all-purpose potatoes, peeled
2 tablespoons margarine or butter
1 pound boneless, skinless chicken breasts (4 pieces)
Butter- or lemon-flavored cooking spray

To make marinade: Combine lemon juice, 2 teaspoons garlic, salt, pepper, 2 teaspoons basil, and 1 teaspoon rosemary in self-sealing plastic bag. Add chicken and seal bag securely. Turn bag several times to coat all areas of chicken with marinade. Refrigerate for 1½ hours. Drain; discard marinade.

While chicken marinates, bring a saucepan of salted water to a boil over high heat; add potatoes. Cook over medium heat for 20 to 25 minutes, or until potatoes can be pierced easily with a fork. Drain and cool. Slice each potato lengthwise into 6 wedges. Place margarine and 1 teaspoon each garlic, basil, and rosemary in a small dish; microwave on high until butter melts. Brush potatoes with flavored margarine and set aside.

Preheat grill according to manufacturer's directions. Spray chicken with cooking spray. Cook for 3 to 8 minutes, or until chicken is slightly firm and juices run clear when it is pierced with a knife. Remove to a serving plate and keep warm.

Place potatoes on grill and cook for 2 to 5 minutes, turning as needed, until golden. Remove to serving dish with chicken. Serve hot.

Outdoor grill: 12 to 14 minutes for chicken, 6 to 8 minutes for potatoes

Hawaiian Chicken With Lime

Makes 4 servings

1 teaspoon grated lime peel
2 tablespoons freshly squeezed lime juice
½ teaspoon curry powder
¼ cup minced fresh cilantro
2 cups nonfat mango yogurt
1 pound boneless, skinless chicken breasts (4 pieces)
Cooking spray
Sliced lime for garnish (optional)

Blend lime peel, juice, curry powder, and cilantro into yogurt. Spoon sauce into a serving bowl. Cover and refrigerate until serving time. Stir sauce before serving.

Preheat grill according to manufacturer's directions. Spray chicken with cooking spray. Grill for 3 to 8 minutes, turning as needed, until chicken is slightly firm to the touch and juices run clear when it is pierced with a knife.

Serve chicken hot, drizzled with yogurt sauce and garnished with lime. This is good with slices of fresh mango, plain or grilled.

Outdoor grill: 12 to 14 minutes

Fettucine With Grilled Chicken, Pecans, and Orange

Makes 4 servings

1 (11-ounce) can mandarin oranges
¼ cup plain nonfat yogurt
¼ cup light mayonnaise
1 teaspoon grated orange peel
¼ cup chopped pecans
12 ounces fresh (refrigerated) fettuccine
1 pound boneless, skinless chicken breasts, cut into
    1-inch wide strips
Garlic-flavored cooking spray
Salt and pepper

Drain mandarin oranges, reserving liquid. Set oranges aside.

To make dressing: Combine yogurt, mayonnaise, reserved mandarin orange juice, and peel in bowl. Cover and refrigerate until needed.

Place pecans on a microwaveable paper towel and microwave on high, stirring once, for 3 to 4 minutes, or until nuts smell toasted. (Or, toast on a baking sheet in a preheated 350-degree oven for 4 to 5 minutes.)

Cook fettuccine in boiling water according to package directions; drain. Place in large bowl. Toss with dressing and mandarin oranges. Set aside.

Preheat grill according to manufacturer's directions. Spray chicken with cooking spray and grill, turning as needed, for 2 to 5 minutes, or until chicken is slightly firm to touch and no longer pink. Remove chicken from grill and season with salt and pepper.

To serve, divide fettuccine and oranges onto 4 plates. Top with chicken, and sprinkle with pecans. Serve warm or cold. This is good with a tossed salad and grilled red onions.

Outdoor grill: 8 to 10 minutes

Greek-Style Chicken Salad

Makes 4 servings

3 tablespoons extra virgin olive oil
Freshly squeezed juice of 2 lemons
2 teaspoons dried oregano
1½ teaspoons dried basil
1 teaspoon minced garlic
Salt and pepper to taste
Olive oil- or lemon-flavored cooking spray
1 pound boneless, skinless chicken breasts, cut into
   1-inch strips
1 (6- to 8-ounce) bag salad mix of your choice
1 medium red onion, sliced thin
2 tomatoes, sliced
¼ cup crumbled feta cheese (optional)

To make dressing: Mix oil, lemon juice, oregano, basil, garlic, salt, and pepper. Set aside. Whisk or shake before serving.

Preheat grill according to manufacturer's directions. Spray grilling surface with cooking spray. Cook chicken strips for 2 to 5 minutes, turning as needed, until no longer pink. Chicken will be slightly firm to touch; do not overcook. Remove from grill and set aside.

Divide and arrange greens on individual salad plates. Arrange onion slices, tomatoes, and chicken strips over greens.

Drizzle dressing over salads. Sprinkle salads with feta cheese if desired. Serve quickly so that the chicken is warm and the salad is cold. This is great with breadsticks.

Outdoor grill: 8 to 10 minutes

Southwest Chicken Salad

Makes 6 servings

2 cups nonfat plain yogurt
2 tablespoons chili powder
1 teaspoon ground cumin
1 teaspoon minced garlic
½ cup chopped cilantro
1 (8- to 10-ounce) bag Romaine lettuce mix
1 red onion, sliced thinly
3 fresh tomatoes, chopped
⅓ cup shredded sharp longhorn Cheddar
Olive oil-flavored cooking spray
2 poblano (or other mild chile) peppers, seeded, cut
    into ½-inch strips
1 pound boneless, skinless chicken breasts, cut into
    1-inch-wide strips
1 cup baked tortilla chips

To make dressing: Combine yogurt, chili powder, cumin, garlic, and cilantro in bowl. Cover and refrigerate until needed.

Place lettuce in large salad bowl. Toss with onion, tomatoes, and cheese.

Preheat grill according to manufacturer's directions. Spray grilling surface with cooking spray. Grill peppers, turning as needed, for 3 to 4 minutes, or until charred all over and slightly softened.

Spray chicken with cooking spray. Grill for 2 to 5 minutes, turning as needed, or until chicken is slightly firm and no longer pink. Remove from grill. Place chicken on salads, and spoon dressing over. Add tortilla chips, and serve. This is good with barbecued or refried beans.

Outdoor grill: 8 to 10 minutes for chicken, 4 to 6 minutes for peppers

California Grilled Chicken Sandwich

Makes 4 servings

1 pound boneless, skinless chicken breasts (4 pieces)
¼ cup extra virgin olive oil
¼ cup freshly squeezed orange juice
1 tablespoon minced garlic
½ teaspoon dried rosemary
¼ teaspoon cayenne
2 tablespoons chopped fresh parsley
Garlic-flavored cooking spray
4 hamburger rolls, sliced
4 leaves lettuce
4 slices tomato
4 slices ripe avocado, dipped in orange juice
1 small red onion, sliced thinly

Place chicken pieces between 2 sheets of waxed paper, and pound with a spatula or mallet to flatten them.

Combine olive oil, orange juice, garlic, rosemary, cayenne, and parsley in a large, self-sealing plastic bag.

Add chicken breasts, close bag securely and turn several times, so that all areas of the chicken are coated by marinade. Refrigerate and marinate 1 hour. Drain, discarding marinade.

Preheat grill according to manufacturer's directions. Spray grilling surface with cooking spray. Cook chicken, turning as needed, for 2 to 7 minutes, or until it is slightly firm to the touch and juices run clear when it is pierced with a knife. Remove chicken from grill.

Arrange lettuce on bottom half of roll. Put chicken on lettuce. Top chicken with tomato, avocado, and onion. Replace top half of roll, and serve.

Outdoor grill: 11 to 13 minutes

Chicken Fajitas

Makes 4 servings

4 green onions, minced
1 teaspoon minced garlic
6 tablespoons dark brown sugar
5 tablespoons red wine vinegar
1½ cups light beer
3 teaspoons prepared mustard
1 pound boneless, skinless chicken breasts, cut into
   1-inch strips
1 onion, sliced
Olive oil-flavored cooking spray
4 flour tortillas
Chopped fresh cilantro

Combine green onions, garlic, sugar, vinegar, beer, and mustard in a saucepan. Simmer 4 to 5 minutes, stirring occasionally. Remove from heat and let cool completely.

Place chicken strips in a shallow glass dish. Pour beer marinade over chicken. Refrigerate and marinate for 1 hour.

Preheat grill according to manufacturer's directions. Cook chicken strips for 2 to 5 minutes, turning as needed, or until slightly firm to the touch and no longer pink. Remove chicken to a plate and keep warm.

Spray onion slices with cooking spray and grill for 2 to 4 minutes, turning as needed, until lightly browned and beginning to soften.

To serve, grill tortillas briefly on each side to warm them. Lay each tortilla flat, place chicken strips in center, and top with onions and a sprinkling of cilantro. Roll tortillas and serve warm. These are good with refried beans and salsa.

Outdoor grill: 8 to 10 minutes for chicken, 6 to 8 minutes for onion slices

Chicken Sausages With Apples and Cucumbers

Makes 4 servings

4 lean chicken sausages (preferably with apple)
Butter-flavored cooking spray
4 firm apples such as Golden Delicious or Granny
    Smith, washed, cored and sliced into rounds
2 cucumbers, peeled and cut lengthwise into pickle-size
    spears
1 teaspoon celery seed

Place sausages in a pan with water to cover. Bring water to a boil, then reduce heat to low and simmer sausages for 10 minutes, or according to package directions. Set aside. (This step can be done ahead of time; refrigerate sausages until you're ready to grill them.)

Preheat grill according to manufacturer's directions. Spray grilling surface with cooking spray. Grill sausages for 2 to 5 minutes or until golden brown on all sides, turning as needed. Remove sausages to a serving plate and keep warm.

Spray apples and cucumbers with cooking spray and grill 3 to 4 minutes, turning as needed, until lightly browned. Remove to serving plate with the sausages and sprinkle with celery seed. Serve hot.

Outdoor grill: 4 to 6 minutes for sausages, 2 to 4 minutes for apples and cucumbers

Note: To be on the safe side, I always recommend cooking sausages before grilling them, to make sure they get cooked through without burning.

Herb-Crusted Turkey

Makes 4 servings

1 cup fine bread crumbs
2 tablespoons minced fresh parsley
½ teaspoon dried basil
½ teaspoon dried tarragon
½ teaspoon dried thyme
¼ teaspoon salt
¼ teaspoon pepper
1 tablespoon olive oil
Butter-flavored cooking spray
1 pound boneless, skinless turkey tenders (breast
   pieces), cut into 4 serving pieces

In a shallow bowl or plate, mix bread crumbs with parsley, basil, tarragon, thyme, salt and pepper, and olive oil.

Spray each piece of turkey with cooking spray. Roll in crumb mixture, patting crumb mixture to help it adhere better to turkey.

Preheat grill according to manufacturer's directions. Spray grilling surface with cooking spray. Grill turkey for 4 to 9 minutes, turning as needed, or until it is slightly firm to the touch and juices run clear when turkey is pierced with a knife. Do not overcook; turkey should still be juicy. Serve hot with grilled vegetables.

Outdoor grill: 12 to 16 minutes

Cajun Turkey Salad

Makes 4 to 6 servings

1 tablespoon dried minced onion
1 teaspoon cayenne
½ teaspoon garlic powder
½ teaspoon dried thyme
½ teaspoon celery salt
½ teaspoon salt
Cooking spray
3 large slices cooked white turkey meat
¼ cup plain nonfat yogurt
¼ cup light mayonnaise
1 onion, chopped
3 cups shredded iceberg lettuce
1 large tomato, chopped

To make Cajun spice mix: Combine dried onion, cayenne, garlic powder, thyme, celery salt, and salt.

Preheat grill according to manufacturer's directions. Spray grilling surface with cooking spray. Sprinkle Cajun spice over turkey slices, then grill turkey for 1 to 3 minutes, turning as needed, just until warmed through and beginning to lightly brown. Remove turkey from grill; dice. Place in bowl. Combine yogurt and mayonnaise. Add to turkey, along with onion, lettuce and tomato, and toss. Serve at room temperature or cold.

Outdoor grill: 2 to 4 minutes

Note: If you prefer not to mix your own spices, you can buy a good-quality Cajun seasoning mix in the supermarket.

Turkey Burgers With Cranberry Relish

Makes 4 servings

3 cups cranberries, picked over, rinsed
2 medium apples, peeled, cored, quartered
1 orange, quartered; discard seeds
¾ to 1 cup sugar, to taste
¼ cup freshly squeezed orange juice
1 pound lean ground turkey (breast meat)
2 egg whites
¼ cup finely ground whole wheat bread crumbs
1 onion, minced
¼ teaspoon ground mace
¼ teaspoon salt
¼ teaspoon pepper
Cooking spray

To make relish: Finely chop cranberries, apples, and orange in a food processor or blender. You may have to do this in two batches. Remove cranberry mixture to a bowl. Stir in sugar and orange juice. Cover and refrigerate overnight. Stir before serving.

Combine ground turkey with egg whites, bread crumbs, onion, mace, salt, and pepper. Shape into 4 patties. Place on a plate and refrigerate until ready to grill.

Preheat grill according to manufacturer's directions. Spray grilling surface with cooking spray. Cook burgers, turning as needed, for 3 to 8 minutes, or until crisp on the outside and cooked through on the inside. Remove burgers to individual plates and serve hot, topped with cranberry relish.

Outdoor grill: 8 to 10 minutes

Sesame Beef

Makes 6 servings

⅓ cup soy sauce
½ cup sake or dry white wine
¾ cup water
4 green onions, minced
1 teaspoon dark sesame oil
1 tablespoon sesame seeds
3 tablespoons sugar
1½ pounds lean sirloin steak
Chili-flavored cooking spray

To make marinade: Combine soy sauce, sake, water, green onions, sesame oil, sesame seeds, and sugar. Divide marinade between 2 large self-sealing plastic bags.

Slice beef against the grain into thin, 2-inch-long strips. Divide meat between the 2 bags. Seal bags and turn a few times to coat the meat. Refrigerate and marinate for 2 to 3 hours, turning bags occasionally. Drain meat.

Preheat grill according to manufacturer's directions. Spray grilling surface with cooking spray. Cook meat in a single layer, turning as needed, for 1 to 4 minutes, or until browned and just cooked through. (Beef can be a bit pink in the middle.) Remove to serving dish. Serve with rice or noodles.

Outdoor grill: 3 to 5 minutes

Peruvian-Style Beef With Tarragon Marinade

Makes 4 servings

¼ cup extra virgin olive oil
1 cup tarragon vinegar
½ cup water
½ teaspoon hot red pepper flakes
1 teaspoon minced garlic
½ teaspoon salt
¼ teaspoon freshly grated black pepper
1 pound lean sirloin steak, cut into 1-inch cubes
6 (8-inch) bamboo skewers, soaked in water 10 min-
     utes, drained

To make marinade: Combine oil, vinegar, water, red pepper, garlic, salt, and pepper. Divide marinade between 2 large self-sealing plastic bags. Add meat, seal bag securely closed and turn 2 to 3 times to coat meat. Refrigerate and marinate 3 to 4 hours. Turn bag once or twice while marinating. Drain, discarding marinade. Thread meat cubes onto skewers.

Preheat grill according to manufacturer's directions. Cook kabobs for 4 to 8 minutes, turning as needed, or until nicely browned outside and cooked to taste inside. This is good served with potatoes or with grilled onions, garlic, or leeks.

Outdoor grill: 9 to 12 minutes

Hamburgers With Olive Salsa

Makes 4 servings

2 medium tomatoes, seeded, chopped
2 teaspoons minced garlic, divided
1 small onion, minced
¼ cup chopped cilantro
Salt and pepper to taste
  cup pitted, chopped green olives
1 pound extra-lean ground beef
Salt and pepper to taste
Olive oil-flavored cooking spray
4 sesame seed hamburger rolls
4 lettuce leaves

To make salsa: Combine tomatoes, 1 teaspoon garlic, onion, cilantro, salt, pepper, and olives in a bowl. Cover and refrigerate until serving time. Toss before serving.

Mix ground beef, 1 teaspoon garlic, salt and pepper. Shape into 4 hamburger patties about ½ inch thick, making hamburgers slightly thinner in middle and thicker on outer edges.

Preheat grill according to manufacturer's directions. Spray grilling surface with cooking spray. Cook hamburgers for 3 to 8 minutes, turning as needed, or until browned on outside and no longer pink inside.

Warm rolls, cut side down, on the grill. Place each roll on a plate. Set a lettuce leaf on the bottom half of roll. Top with a burger and a spoonful of salsa. Replace top half of roll. Serve hamburgers hot with remaining salsa on the side.

Outdoor grill: 8 to 10 minutes

Lamb Kabobs With Balsamic Marinade

Makes 4 servings

⅓ cup extra virgin olive oil

¼ cup balsamic vinegar

1 teaspoon minced garlic

1 teaspoon dried rosemary

¼ teaspoon salt

¼ teaspoon freshly ground black pepper

1 pound lean leg or sirloin of lamb, trimmed of all fat
   and cut into 1-inch cubes

2 medium onions, cut in quarters

2 green peppers, cut into 16 pieces

8 cherry tomatoes

4 bamboo skewers, soaked in water for 10 minutes and
   drained

Make the marinade: Combine oil, vinegar, garlic, rosemary, salt, and pepper.

Thread lamb cubes alternately on skewers with onion quarters, pepper pieces, and cherry tomatoes. Arrange skewers in a shallow glass dish. Pour marinade over kabobs and refrigerate for 4 to 6 hours, turning occasionally. When ready to grill, drain marinade.

Preheat grill according to manufacturer's directions. Cook kabobs, turning as needed, 4 to 8 minutes, or until lamb is brown on outside and done to taste on inside. Remove skewers to serving dish. This is good with rice pilaf or couscous.

Outdoor grill: 9 to 12 minutes

Note: If using a contact grill that does not open flat, leave out the cherry tomatoes, which would get squished, and use more onions and peppers.

Mexican Barbecue

Makes 4 servings

1 pound pork tenderloin
4 red or green bell peppers
1 large red onion, cut into 6 slices
½ teaspoon black pepper
½ teaspoon ground cumin
½ teaspoon minced garlic
2 tablespoons canola oil blend

Cut pork across the grain into ½-inch-thick slices. Seed peppers and slice lengthwise into quarters. Mix pepper, cumin, and garlic into the oil.

Preheat grill according to manufacturer's directions. Brush pork with flavored oil. Grill pork slices for 3 to 7 minutes, turning as needed, or until browned on outside and just cooked through inside. Place pork on serving dish and keep warm. Grill peppers and onion slices about 2 to 4 minutes, turning as needed, or until lightly charred and slightly softened. Place on serving platter with pork. This is good with warm tortillas and sliced oranges on the side.

Outdoor grill: 8 to 10 minutes for pork, 6 to 8 minutes for peppers

Pork Kabobs With Peach Glaze

Makes 4 servings

2 cups peach juice (nectar)
2 tablespoons cornstarch
½ teaspoon curry powder
½ teaspoon ground cinnamon
½ teaspoon chili powder
½ teaspoon ground allspice
4 bamboo skewers, soaked in water 10 minutes, drained
4 peaches, pitted and cut into quarters
4 green onions, cut into 2-inch lengths
2 green bell peppers, seeded, cut into 2-inch pieces
1 pound pork tenderloin, cut into 1-inch cubes
Cooking spray

Mix 3 tablespoons of the peach nectar with cornstarch. Heat remaining peach juice to a boil in saucepan. Mix in curry powder, cinnamon, chili powder, and allspice. Add cornstarch mixture. Reduce heat and simmer about 4 to 5 minutes or until sauce thickens. Remove from heat. Set aside.

Thread skewers alternately with pieces of peach, green onions, pepper, and pork cubes. Brush each kabob generously with peach glaze.

Preheat grill according to manufacturer's directions. Spray grilling surface with cooking spray. Grill kabobs, turning as needed, for 4 to 8 minutes, or until pork is slightly firm to the touch and cooked through. Remove kabobs to serving dish. Serve hot with noodles or rice.

Outdoor grill: 9 to 12 minutes

Pork With Pineapple and Lichees

Makes 4 servings

2 teaspoons canola blend oil
1½ teaspoons minced ginger, divided
3 tablespoons soy sauce
3 tablespoons dry white wine, or chicken broth
½ cup canned, drained lichees
½ cup canned pineapple chunks packed in juice,
   drained; reserve ½ cup juice
2 tablespoons cornstarch
Cooking spray
1 pound pork tenderloin, cut into ½-inch-thick slices

To make the sauce: Heat oil with ginger in a saucepan. Stir in soy sauce and white wine or broth. Stir in lichees and pineapple chunks. Mix 3 tablespoons of reserved pineapple juice with cornstarch. Add remaining juice to lichee mixture. Then blend cornstarch mixture into sauce. Continue cooking over medium heat, stirring, until sauce thickens slightly. Set aside.

Preheat grill according to manufacturer's directions. Spray grilling surface and pork with cooking spray. Place pork on grill and sprinkle with ½ teaspoon ginger. Cook pork for 3 to 7 minutes, turning as needed, or until pork is firm and just cooked through. Remove pork to a plate and spoon sauce over it. Serve at once, with any remaining lichees and pineapple on the side. This is good with rice or noodles.

Outdoor grill: 8 to 10 minutes

Note: Canned lichees are available in Asian food markets and some supermarkets. If you cannot get them, substitute an additional ½ cup of pineapple chunks.

Fish and Seafood

Lean and quick-cooking, fish and shellfish not only are good choices if you're watching your weight and/or cholesterol, but they also taste fabulous grilled.

Firm-textured fish hold up well on the grill; they don't fall apart, and can be used for kabobs. They include such full-flavored favorites as catfish, grouper, ono, shark, swordfish, salmon, and tuna.

At the other end of the spectrum are thin, delicate fish that will fall apart with overhandling. Cover the grill if possible, and don't turn the fish any more than necessary during cooking. Fish that need gentle handling include cod, sole, flounder, scrod, perch, and whitefish.

"All-thumbs" cooks will be happy to know there's an actual rule for cooking fish: 10 minutes per inch of thickness. Just eyeball the thickness (or measure it, if you prefer precision), and allow the proper amount of time. Thin fillets generally cook in 2 to 5 minutes; thicker fillets and steaks can take up to 8 to 12 minutes. These cooking times may be shorter on a contact grill, which cooks both sides of the fish at once.

Tips for buying, preparing and grilling fish

• Fillets are cut lengthwise from the side of the fish, and except for a stray bone or two, are usually sold boneless. They are thin and cook quickly, making them ideal for indoor grills. Put them skin side down on the grid. If you have a grill with a cover, you don't need to turn fillets unless they're thick.

• Steaks are cut crosswise, and are usually at least ¾ inch thick. Just about any fish sold in steak form is firm enough to hold up well on the grill. Steaks do have some bones, along the inside curve. If you're grilling fish steaks on an open grill, they should be turned once.

• Kabobs are ¾- to 1½-inch cubes cut from fish steaks. You can cut them yourself, or sometimes buy them already made into kabobs. You can cut kabobs from fillets, but they'll be thin and you'll probably need to thread the skewer through them in two or three places.

• Fresh fish spoils quickly. Use it within a day—two days, tops—of buying it. Use shellfish within one day. Frozen, raw fish will keep for one to six months. Plan to use frozen fish with a high fat content, such as salmon, within a month or two. Don't refreeze fish once it has been thawed; refreezing ruins the texture.

• Always keep fish and shellfish refrigerated until the grill is ready, and thaw frozen fish in its wrapper in the refrigerator. Thawing will take from 5 to 24 hours, depending on the thickness of the fish. Never thaw fish at room temperature. If necessary, you can thaw the fish quickly by placing it, still tightly wrapped, in cold water. If it's wrapped in paper, put it in a plastic bag first to keep the water from flooding it. It will take about 1 hour per pound to thaw it by this method; refresh the water every 30 minutes. You can cook thin fillets of fish that are still frozen, as long as you allow some extra time.

• Fish, especially the skin, has a tendency to stick to grill surfaces. If the fish is not marinated or the marinade contains no oil, spray both the fish and the grill surface with cooking spray, or brush them lightly with oil.

• Fish fillets and steaks have sections, or flakes, marked by faint lines in the flesh. When the fish is done, these sections will separate—that is, the fish will "flake"—when you gently prod the fish with a fork. The sections should gently separate; if the fish falls into pieces and no longer looks moist, it's overcooked.

• If you grow your own herbs, you can make kabobs with pizzazz by using woody herb stems as skewers for fish cubes, shrimp, or scallops. Tarragon and rosemary work well for this. Strip the leaves from the stem. Using a small, sharp knife, cut a point at one end of the stem. Thread the seafood onto the stem, and grill.

• Mollusks such as oysters, clams, and mussels really require a covered grill and high heat, which makes them a better bet for an outdoor grill turned on "high" (or with hot coals) than for that little countertop number.

• If you're cooking mollusks and small crustaceans such as shrimp on a gas grill, you might want to put them on a grill screen so they don't fall between the wires of the cooking grid. Cook them over as high heat as possible so they cook through before they turn rubbery. You want them to stay plump and juicy.

Grilled Tuna Salad Mediterranean Style

Makes 4 servings

1 pound fresh tuna, cut into ¾-inch-wide strips
Garlic-flavored cooking spray
1 cup boiled potatoes, diced
1 onion, chopped
1 green bell pepper, seeded and chopped
1 cup cooked, drained green beans
¼ cup light mayonnaise
¼ cup plain nonfat yogurt
½ teaspoon dried basil
½ teaspoon minced garlic
½ teaspoon salt
½ teaspoon black pepper
4 lettuce leaves
1 tomato, sliced

Preheat grill according to manufacturer's directions. Spray tuna with cooking spray. Cook tuna strips 3 to 7 minutes, turning as needed, or until tuna is firm to the touch and opaque. Do not overcook. Remove tuna to mixing bowl. Flake into small chunks. Mix in potatoes, onion, bell pepper, and beans. Mix together mayonnaise, yogurt, basil, garlic, salt, and pepper. Add to salad and toss lightly.

Arrange lettuce leaf on each of 4 plates. Spoon tuna salad onto lettuce leaf; garnish with tomato.

Serve warm or cold with French bread.

Outdoor grill: 7 to 8 minutes

Seafood Spinach Pasta Salad

Makes 8 servings

½ cup extra virgin olive oil
¼ cup balsamic vinegar
¼ teaspoon paprika
¼ teaspoon dry mustard
1 teaspoon minced garlic
3 tablespoons minced fresh dillweed
Salt and pepper to taste
1 package (1 pound) spinach pasta
1 medium red onion, sliced thinly
1 medium zucchini, cut in half lengthwise
Olive oil–flavored cooking spray
¾ pound haddock fillets (or fish of your choice)
½ pound sea scallops
½ pound shredded crab meat (real or imitation)

To make dressing: Blend oil and vinegar in bowl. Mix in ingredients through salt and pepper. Cover and refrigerate. Whisk before serving.

Cook pasta according to package directions; drain. Place in bowl. Toss with red onion and a little of the dressing. Set aside.

Preheat grill according to manufacturer's directions. Spray cut side of zucchini with cooking spray. Grill 3 to 6 minutes, turning as needed, until lightly browned. Slice and add to pasta.

Spray haddock fillets and scallops with cooking spray. Grill haddock and scallops 3 to 6 minutes, turning as needed, until haddock is opaque and flakes easily, and scallops are cooked through. Flake haddock and add to salad along with scallops and crab. Add dressing to taste. Serve warm or cold.

Outdoor grill: 5 to 8 minutes for fish and scallops, 6 to 7 minutes for zucchini

Note: You can substitute bottled low-fat salad dressing for the homemade dressing.

Salmon With Minted Tomato Salsa

Makes 4 servings

4 large ripe tomatoes
¼ cup plus 1 teaspoon finely chopped fresh mint leaves
3 tablespoons finely chopped fresh cilantro
3 green onions, minced
1 tablespoon extra virgin olive oil
¼ cup freshly squeezed lemon juice
¼ teaspoon minced garlic
Salt and black pepper
1 pound salmon fillets, cut into 4 serving pieces
Olive oil-flavored cooking spray

Cut tomatoes in half. Squeeze tomatoes and discard seeds. Chop tomatoes and place in bowl. Add ¼ cup mint, cilantro, green onions, olive oil, lemon juice, garlic, and salt and pepper to taste. Allow salsa to stand for 30 minutes at room temperature. (Refrigerate for longer storage.) Toss before serving. Taste to adjust seasonings.

Spray salmon with cooking spray. Sprinkle with 1 teaspoon mint and ¼ teaspoon black pepper. Preheat grill. Cook salmon for 4 to 8 minutes, turning as needed, or until fish flakes easily when prodded with a fork. Total cooking time will depend on the thickness of the fish pieces.

Remove salmon to a platter and serve immediately with mint-tomato salsa. This is good with pasta or couscous.

Outdoor grill: 7 to 10 minutes

Pepper-Crusted Salmon Steaks

Makes 4 servings

1½ teaspoons crushed black peppercorns
1½ teaspoons crushed white peppercorns (or, use all
  black peppercorns)
1 tablespoon minced ginger
4 small salmon steaks, each about ¾ inch thick, washed
  and patted dry
Butter-flavored cooking spray
2 cups tangerine slices, for garnish (optional)

Mix peppercorns and ginger together in a small bowl. Set aside.

Spray salmon with cooking spray. Sprinkle peppercorn mixture onto salmon steaks, coating both sides. Pat spice mixture firmly onto salmon to help it adhere.

Preheat grill according to manufacturer's directions. Spray grilling surface with cooking spray. Cook salmon for 4 to 8 minutes, turning as needed, or until fish flakes easily when prodded with a fork but is still moist inside.

Remove salmon steaks to serving dishes. Garnish with tangerine slices if desired. Serve hot.

Outdoor grill: 7 to 8 minutes

Swordfish or Halibut With Grilled Fresh Figs

Makes 4 servings

1 pound small swordfish or halibut steaks
4 to 6 ripe fresh figs, cut in half lengthwise
Butter-flavored cooking spray

Preheat grill according to manufacturer's directions. Spray fish steaks and cut sides of figs with cooking spray.

Grill fish for 5 to 10 minutes, turning as needed, or until fish is opaque and flakes easily. Cooking time will depend on thickness of fish. If necessary, cut fish into 4 serving pieces.

Spray grilling surface with cooking spray. Grill figs for 3 to 4 minutes, or until warmed through.

Remove fish and figs to a serving plate. Serve immediately.

Outdoor grill: 8 to 10 minutes for fish, 4 to 5 minutes for figs

Note: You can brush figs lightly with a no-sugar-added jam before grilling.

Orange Roughy With Pineapple

Makes 4 servings

1 small fresh peeled, cored, and sliced pineapple, drained
¼ cup brown sugar, or to taste
Butter-flavored cooking spray
1 pound orange roughy fillets, in 4 pieces (or use
  snapper)
Salt and pepper to taste

Place pineapple slices on a plate and sprinkle with brown sugar.

Preheat grill according to manufacturer's directions. Spray grilling surface with cooking spray. Grill pineapple slices 2 to 4 minutes, turning as needed, until warm and lightly browned. Remove to a plate and set aside.

Spray fish fillets with cooking spray. Cook fish for 2 to 5 minutes, turning as needed, until fish is opaque and flakes easily when prodded with a fork. Remove each fillet to a plate; sprinkle with salt and pepper. Serve with grilled pineapple.

Outdoor grill: 4 to 6 minutes for fish, 2 to 4 minutes for pineapple

Note: Peeled and cored fresh pineapple is available in most supermarket produce departments, but if you cannot find it, buy a whole pineapple. Choose one that has green leaves and that is not too soft. Trim off the leaf end, then use a small, sharp knife to cut off the peel. Cut into slices about ½ inch thick, then use the small knife to cut out the woody core.

Grouper Sandwich With Horseradish Sauce

Makes 4 servings

1 tablespoon canola or canola blend oil

1 medium onion, minced

1 cup light beer

3 tablespoons cider vinegar

½ teaspoon dry mustard

¼ teaspoon black pepper

¼ teaspoon ground cumin

Cooking spray

4 hamburger rolls, split

4 lettuce leaves

2 tablespoons ground white horseradish

1 cup plain nonfat yogurt

4 grouper fillets, about 6 ounces each

4 large slices tomato

To make the marinade: Heat oil in saucepan. Cook onion for 4 minutes over medium heat, stirring occasionally. Stir in beer, vinegar, mustard, pepper, and cumin. Cool completely. Pour marinade into large, self-sealing plastic bag. Slide in grouper and seal bag securely. Turn bag several times, so that all surfaces of fish are coated by marinade. Refrigerate and marinate for 2 hours, turning several times. Remove fish from marinade; discard marinade.

Preheat grill according to manufacturer's directions. Spray grilling surface with cooking spray. Place rolls on grill, cut side down, for a minute or two to toast them. (Do not toast on closed contact grill.) Set rolls on plates. Place a lettuce leaf on each open roll. Mix horseradish with yogurt in a bowl.

Spray fish fillets and cook for 3 to 6 minutes, or until fish is opaque and flakes easily when prodded with a fork. Set grouper on lettuce-lined rolls. Top with tomato. Pass horseradish sauce and pickles at the table.

Outdoor grill: 4 to 6 minutes

Cornmeal-Crusted Catfish

Makes 4 servings

1 cup evaporated skim milk
2 cups cornmeal, preferably white
½ teaspoon paprika
¼ teaspoon dried sage
¼ teaspoon dried thyme
¼ teaspoon salt
¼ teaspoon black pepper
4 catfish fillets, about 6 ounces each
Cooking spray

Pour milk into a shallow bowl.

Mix together cornmeal, paprika, sage, thyme, salt, and pepper. Spread on a plate. Dip fish in milk. Drain. Roll catfish fillets in cornmeal mixture. Set catfish on a plate and refrigerate until serving time.

Preheat grill according to manufacturer's directions. Spray grilling surface with cooking spray. Cook catfish for 3 to 6 minutes, turning as needed, or until coating is crusty and fish flakes when prodded with a fork.

Remove fish and set on individual plates. This is good with coleslaw and/or Sweet Potato Chips (Page 79).

Outdoor grill: 4 to 6 minutes

Rainbow Trout With Parsley and Dill

Makes 2 servings

2 cleaned rainbow trout, about 8 ounces each
½ cup parsley sprigs, washed
½ cup fresh dillweed
1 lemon, cut into 6 thin slices
Butter-flavored cooking spray
Lemon pepper
Additional parsley for garnish

Wash trout and pat dry with paper towels. Arrange parsley, dill, and 2 slices of lemon in the cavity of each fish. Spray the fish with cooking spray and sprinkle with lemon pepper.

Preheat grill according to manufacturer's directions. Spray grilling surface with cooking spray. Cook trout, turning as needed, for 8 to 15 minutes, or until fish is opaque and flakes easily when prodded with a fork.

Place 1 trout on each of 2 plates. Serve with additional parsley and remaining lemon slices. This is good with a tossed salad and lemon blueberry muffins.

Outdoor grill: 12 to 15 minutes

Trout With Almonds and Oranges

Makes 4 servings

4 trout fillets
Butter-flavored cooking spray
Salt and pepper to taste
2 oranges, sliced (leave peel on)
½ cup chopped roasted almonds

Spray trout fillets with cooking spray and sprinkle with salt and pepper.

Preheat grill according to manufacturer's directions. Spray grilling surface with cooking spray. Cook trout 2 to 8 minutes, turning as needed, until fish is opaque and flakes easily when prodded with a fork. Cooking time will vary according to thickness of fillets. Place fish on individual dinner plates.

Spray orange slices with cooking spray and grill 2 to 4 minutes, turning as needed, until warmed and lightly browned. Arrange on plates with trout. Sprinkle trout and oranges with almonds. Serve immediately.

Outdoor grill: 4 to 8 minutes for fish, 4 to 6 minutes for oranges

Whitefish and Green Onions

Makes 4 servings

½ cup low-fat or fat-free Caesar salad dressing
4 whitefish fillets, about 6 ounces each
8 green onions, trimmed
Olive oil-flavored cooking spray

Pour dressing into self-sealing plastic bag. Add fish and green onions. Seal bag securely closed. Turn bag several times so that all surfaces of fish and onions are coated by marinade. Refrigerate and marinate for 1 hour, turning once. Drain whitefish. Separate onions.

Preheat grill according to manufacturer's directions. Spray grilling surface with cooking spray. Cook whitefish about 3 to 5 minutes, turning as needed, until fish flakes easily when prodded with a fork. Remove each piece to an individual dish. Grill onions for 1 to 4 minutes, turning as needed. Arrange 2 onions on each piece of whitefish. Serve hot. This is good with a tossed salad and croutons, or grilled zucchini (Page 74).

Outdoor grill: 4 to 5 minutes for fish, 5 to 6 minutes for onions

Anise-Marinated Flounder With Fresh Asparagus

Makes 4 servings

½ cup dry white wine
¼ cup olive oil
½ teaspoon anise seeds
3 tablespoons minced fresh parsley
4 flounder fillets, about 6 ounces each
1 pound thin asparagus, washed and trimmed
Olive oil–flavored cooking spray

Combine wine, olive oil, anise seeds, and parsley. Pour marinade into self-sealing plastic bag. Add flounder fillets and seal bag securely closed. Turn bag several times so that all surfaces of fish are coated by marinade. Refrigerate and marinate for 1 hour, turning once. Drain, discarding marinade.

Preheat grill according to manufacturer's directions. Cook flounder for 1½ to 4 minutes, turning as needed, or until fish flakes easily when prodded with a fork. Remove flounder to serving dish and keep warm.

Spray asparagus with cooking spray. Grill for 2 to 5 minutes, turning as needed, until just cooked through but still crisp. Arrange on dish with fish and serve immediately. This is good with warm garlic bread.

Outdoor grill: 3 to 4 minutes for flounder, 4 to 6 minutes for asparagus

Shrimp With Salsa Verde

Makes 4 servings

1 tablespoon white vinegar
1 teaspoon sugar
2 teaspoons minced garlic
¼ teaspoon salt
2 medium cucumbers, peeled, seeded and chopped
4 fresh tomatillos, husked and finely chopped, or 4
    canned, drained tomatillos
¼ teaspoon red pepper flakes, or to taste
¼ cup finely chopped fresh cilantro
Olive oil-flavored cooking spray
1½ pounds peeled, deveined and washed large raw
    shrimp
Salt, pepper, and garlic powder to taste

To make salsa: Place vinegar, sugar, garlic, and salt in a glass bowl. Add cucumbers, tomatillos, red pepper flakes, and cilantro. Cover and refrigerate until needed. Stir before using. You will have about 2 cups of salsa.

Preheat grill according to manufacturer's directions. Spray grilling surface with cooking spray. Spray shrimp with cooking spray and sprinkle with salt, pepper, and garlic powder. Grill shrimp 1½ to 4 minutes, turning as needed, or until opaque and slightly firm. Do not overcook, or shrimp will be tough.

Set shrimp on plates and spoon a little salsa verde over them. Pass extra salsa at the table. This is good with brown rice and grilled tomatoes.

Outdoor grill: 4 to 6 minutes

Note: Many supermarkets carry fresh tomatillos, which look like small green tomatoes in husks, but if you cannot find them fresh, look for canned tomatillos in the Hispanic foods aisle.

Butterflied Shrimp in Beer With Barbecue Sauce

Makes 4 servings

1½ pounds extra large raw shrimp, peeled, deveined,
   and washed
1 (12-ounce) can light beer
½ cup (or as needed) Tangy Barbecue Sauce (Page 95),
   or your favorite bottled barbecue sauce
2 green onions (both white and green parts), trimmed
   and minced
Butter-flavored cooking spray
Salt and paprika

To butterfly shrimp, cut lengthwise down the shrimp, cutting most, but not all of the way, through the shrimp. This will allow them to lie flat. Place shrimp in a glass bowl and pour beer over them. Let marinate for 2 to 4 hours in the refrigerator, turning occasionally. Drain.

In a small glass bowl, combine barbecue sauce and green onions. Set aside.

Preheat grill according to manufacturer's directions. Spray grilling surface with cooking spray. Brush shrimp lightly with barbecue sauce and sprinkle with salt and paprika. Grill shrimp for 1 to 3 minutes, turning as needed and brushing once or twice with sauce, until opaque and slightly firm. Do not overcook shrimp or they will be tough. Serve hot, with coleslaw and plenty of good bread.

Outdoor grill: 3 to 5 minutes

Note: You can buy frozen shrimp already peeled and deveined. Thaw it in the refrigerator. If you buy shrimp in the shell, peel off the legs and shell with your fingers. With a small, sharp knife, cut lengthwise down the back of the shrimp and remove the vein.

Slimmer Shrimp "Po Boys"

Makes 4 servings

4 individual French bread rolls, cut in half lengthwise
Butter-flavored cooking spray
2 cups fine yellow cornmeal
¼ teaspoon salt
¼ teaspoon red pepper flakes
¼ teaspoon paprika
¼ teaspoon garlic powder
2 egg whites, lightly beaten
1½ pounds extra-large shrimp, peeled, deveined
4 lettuce leaves, washed and dried
2 tablespoons light mayonnaise
1 small red onion, chopped
3 tablespoons chopped sweet pickle
2 medium tomatoes, sliced

Spray cut sides of rolls with cooking spray; set aside.

Spread cornmeal on plate. Mix in salt, red pepper, paprika, and garlic.

Preheat grill according to manufacturer's directions. Spray grilling surface with cooking spray. Roll shrimp in egg whites, then in cornmeal mixture. Grill shrimp 1½ to 4 minutes, turning as needed, or just until opaque.

Place rolls on grill, cut sides down, and grill for 1 minute or until warm and lightly toasted. (Do not toast on a closed contact grill.)

Place a lettuce leaf on the top half of each roll. Mix mayonnaise with onion and pickle. Spread mixture on bottom half of each roll. Top with shrimp, then tomato. Replace tops to sandwiches and serve immediately.

Outdoor grill: 4 to 6 minutes

Note: Grilling, rather than deep-frying, the seafood in this classic New Orleans favorite cuts the amount of fat considerably.

Shrimp Burritos

Makes 6 servings

1½ pounds peeled, deveined large shrimp
Garlic-flavored cooking spray
Ground cumin
Dried oregano
1 medium onion, sliced ¼ inch thick
6 flour tortillas
1 small avocado, pitted and cut lengthwise into 6
    wedges
Fresh Tomato Salsa (Page 92), or bottled salsa

Preheat grill according to manufacturer's directions. Spray grilling surface with cooking spray. Spray shrimp with cooking spray and sprinkle lightly with cumin and oregano. Grill 1½ to 4 minutes, turning as needed, or until shrimp is opaque and slightly firm. Do not overcook. Remove to a plate and keep warm.

Spray onion slices with cooking spray. Grill for 1 to 3 minutes, turning as needed, or until lightly browned. Remove to plate with shrimp.

Warm tortillas, one at a time, on the grill for just a few seconds.

Arrange shrimp, onion slices, and avocado wedges down center of each tortilla, leaving room at each end. Fold one side of tortilla over filling, tuck in ends, and fold other side over. Place on plates, folded side down.

Serve burritos immediately, with salsa. These are good with refried beans.

Outdoor grill: 4 to 6 minutes for shrimp, 4 to 6 minutes for onions

Chile Sea Scallop Kabobs

Makes 4 servings

1 tablespoon canola blend oil
1 medium onion, minced
½ teaspoon minced ginger
½ teaspoon minced garlic
Hot red pepper flakes
¼ cup soy sauce
2 tablespoons light brown sugar
3 tablespoons chile paste with garlic, available at Asian
  food stores (see note)
3 tablespoons red wine vinegar
12 large sea scallops
24 snow peas, trimmed
12 (8-inch) bamboo skewers, soaked in water 10 minutes, drained
Cooking spray

To prepare sauce, heat oil in a pan. Add onion, ginger, garlic, and red pepper and cook for 2 minutes, stirring often. Add soy sauce, brown sugar, chile paste, and vinegar. Simmer 1 minute to combine ingredients.

Thread scallops and snow peas alternately onto skewers. Brush with sauce.

Preheat grill according to manufacturer's directions. Spray grilling surface with cooking spray. Grill kabobs over medium heat, turning once or twice during grilling or as needed, and brushing once with sauce. Cook 3 to 6 minutes, or until scallops are firm and opaque, but still moist. Remove kabobs from grill and serve 3 to each person, with plain or fried rice. (If making this as an appetizer rather than a main course, allow 1 kabob per person.)

Outdoor grill: 6 to 8 minutes

Note: You could substitute spicy ketchup or hot salsa for the chile paste.

Sea Scallops With Tomato And Tarragon

Makes 4 servings

2 large, ripe tomatoes
1 tablespoon extra virgin olive oil
2 teaspoons freshly squeezed lemon juice
1 tablespoon minced fresh tarragon, or 1½ teaspoons
   dried
Salt and pepper to taste
¼ teaspoon pepper
1¼ pounds sea scallops
Olive oil–flavored cooking spray

To make sauce, cut tomatoes, squeeze out seeds and chop. Place tomatoes in a colander and drain for 5 minutes. Put chopped tomatoes in a bowl. Mix in olive oil, lemon juice, tarragon, and salt and pepper. Cover tightly and refrigerate until serving time. Just before serving, toss sauce. Taste to adjust seasonings. Spoon chopped tomato mixture onto plates.

Spray scallops with cooking spray. Preheat grill according to manufacturer's directions. Grill scallops for 3 to 6 minutes, turning as needed, or until firm and opaque, but still moist. Remove from grill and set on tomato sauce. Serve hot. These are good with sliced cucumbers and pasta shells.

Outdoor grill: 6 to 8 minutes

Breaded Soft-Shelled Crabs

Makes 4 servings

2 cups fine bread crumbs
½ teaspoon dried oregano
½ teaspoon dried basil
1 tablespoon minced fresh parsley
¼ teaspoon salt
⅛ teaspoon pepper
1 tablespoon butter or margarine, melted
2 tablespoons extra virgin olive oil
8 soft-shelled crabs, cleaned
Olive oil-flavored cooking spray

Mix bread crumbs with oregano, basil, parsley, salt, and pepper. Spread in a flat dish. Set aside.

Combine melted butter and olive oil and pour into a shallow bowl. Reserve.

Brush crabs with oil-butter mixture and then dust each crab with bread crumb mixture, patting crumbs to help them stick.

Preheat grill according to manufacturer's directions. Spray grilling surface with cooking spray. Cook crabs for 4 to 7 minutes, turning as needed, or until they turn red. Serve with a tossed salad or potato salad, and garlic bread.

Outdoor grill: 6 to 7 minutes

Note: Soft-shelled crabs are sold live and are very perishable. Have the fishmonger clean them for you, and cook them the same day you buy them. People who have never tried this delicious seafood are surprised to learn that you eat the whole crab, shell and all!

Fruits, Vegetables, Grains

You've heard it over and over again: One of the keys to a healthy diet is to eat more fruits, vegetables, and grains.

Grilling makes this "task" easy, even delightful. The high, dry heat of grilling brings out the sweetness in vegetables and infuses them with a slightly smoky flavor. And what it does to fruit is nothing short of wonderful. Dessert, anyone?

It is always a surprise to many cooks that soft fruits such as melon, pineapple and bananas, and vegetables such as eggplant slices, peppers, cucumbers, mushrooms, and summer squash, all grill well. Some manufacturers recommend a lower heat for these foods. When we tested them, they cooked on medium-high heat for a very few minutes. But again, the timing depends on your machine.

Don't forget legumes and grains. Obviously you can't cook rice or baked beans directly on the grill, but firm tofu does fine on the grill. So does polenta, the molded cornmeal mixture that's a good alternative to pasta. And the grill is a good way to quickly toast bread or hamburger buns, or warm tortillas. Toasting bread can take only seconds; watch it carefully, especially if your grill has only one heat setting, so that the bread doesn't burn.

Buying, preparing, and grilling fruits and vegetables

• Always buy the freshest produce possible. Farmers markets are great places to buy fruits and vegetables at the height of their season.

• Vegetables usually don't need marinating, although I do call for marinades in some recipes to add flavor.

• For really soft vegetables such as tomatoes, you'll need to cook on an open grill. If you have a contact (two-sided) grill, open it up to a flat surface (if your grill does that) when cooking such foods as tomatoes or figs. If your grill can't be used flat, skip the soft foods.

• Although potatoes and sweet potatoes can be sliced and cooked directly on the grill for a long time, I find I have better luck if I boil them first, then grill them just long enough to brown them. To save some time, you can microwave rather than boil them—allow about 6 to 8 minutes on "high" for a medium-size potato.

• Because they do contain sugars, fruits and vegetables can burn easily and take on an acrid flavor—not to mention leave a trail of burnt sugar on the grill surface. Watch them carefully; most need to cook only a short time.

• I assume most people will serve the vegetables or grains as side dishes, and have figured serving sizes accordingly. Many of these dishes, however, make excellent vegetarian main courses. If you are serving them as a main course, figure on half as many servings as the recipe allows.

Stuffed Sweet Peppers, Chinese Style

Makes 12 stuffed pepper pieces

6 ounces lean ground pork
1 green onion, minced
2 teaspoons minced ginger
2 tablespoons minced water chestnuts
2 tablespoons dry sherry
4 tablespoons soy sauce, divided
¼ teaspoon salt
3 red or green bell peppers, seeded and cut into quarters lengthwise
½ cup water
1 teaspoon sugar
4 tablespoons cornstarch
Cooking spray

Mix together pork, green onion, ginger, water chestnuts, sherry, 1 tablespoon soy sauce, and salt in a bowl. Set aside. For easy preparation, these ingredients can be minced together in a food processor fitted with a steel blade.

Press pork mixture evenly over cut sides of peppers. Spread cornstarch in a flat dish and press stuffed side into cornstarch. Tap off excess cornstarch. Place peppers on dish and set aside.

Prepare a sauce by combining 3 tablespoons soy sauce, water, and sugar in a small saucepan. Cook over medium heat until sugar dissolves, about 3 minutes. Set aside.

Preheat grill according to manufacturer's directions. Spray grilling surface with cooking spray. Place pepper pieces on grill, stuffed side down. Grill for 2 to 4 minutes, turning as needed, or until stuffing is crisp on the outside and no longer pink inside. Remove stuffed peppers to serving dish and drizzle with sauce. Serve hot.

Outdoor grill: 6 to 8 minutes

Grilled Pepper Salad

Makes 6 servings

3 green, red and/or yellow bell peppers
Olive oil-flavored cooking spray
2 tablespoons red wine vinegar
1 tablespoon balsamic vinegar (regular or white)
¼ cup olive oil, preferably extra virgin
1 teaspoon dried marjoram
2 tablespoons capers, drained

Cut peppers in half lengthwise, remove cores and seeds, and cut lengthwise again into ½-inch-wide strips. Spray with cooking spray.

Preheat grill according to manufacturer's directions. Grill peppers about 2 to 4 minutes, turning as necessary, or until lightly charred and slightly softened. Put in a salad bowl.

Whisk together vinegars, oil, and marjoram. Toss with peppers. Add capers, and toss again. Serve warm or cold.

Outdoor grill: 4 to 6 minutes

Note: If the skin on the peppers is charred enough to loosen, you can remove it. Place hot grilled peppers in a heavy plastic bag for a few minutes, then take them out of the bag and rub them gently with a paper towel to remove most of the skin.

Corn and Pepper Salad

Makes 4 servings

Butter-flavored cooking spray
4 ears of corn, silks and husks removed
Salt and pepper to taste
1 large green or red bell pepper, seeded and chopped
5 green onions, trimmed, minced, including most of
    green tops
3 tablespoons imitation bacon bits
3 tablespoons balsamic vinegar
2 tablespoons extra virgin olive oil, or to taste

Preheat grill according to manufacturer's directions. Spray grilling surface with cooking spray. Spray corn and grill about 5 to 8 minutes, turning as needed, until lightly charred.

Cool corn. Using a small sharp knife, carefully, strip corn from the cob on a cutting board. Put corn in a bowl. Season with salt and pepper. Mix in pepper, onions, bacon bits, vinegar, and oil.

Cover and refrigerate until serving time. Serve at room temperature.

Outdoor grill: 4 to 6 minutes; for best results, cut each ear of corn crosswise into 3 pieces before grilling

Note: You cannot grill corn on a contact grill unless the grill can be opened flat.

Grilled Golden Corn With Toasted Tortilla Chips

Makes 4 servings

¼ cup grated fresh Parmesan cheese

1 teaspoon poppy seeds

½ teaspoon salt

½ teaspoon ground cumin

5 corn or flour tortillas, each cut into 6 to 8 wedges (chips)

Butter- or olive oil-flavored cooking spray

4 ears of corn, silks and husks removed

Salt and pepper to taste

In a small bowl combine the cheese, poppy seeds, salt, and cumin. Spray tortilla chips with cooking spray. Preheat grill according to manufacturer's directions. Spray grilling surface with cooking spray. Cook tortilla pieces for about 30 seconds on each side, until lightly toasted. Set chips on a plate and sprinkle with cheese mixture while chips are still warm.

Spray corn with cooking spray. Spray grilling surface again with cooking spray. Cook corn about 5 to 7 minutes, rotating as necessary. Remove corn to individual plates. Sprinkle with salt and pepper and serve hot, accompanied by tortilla chips.

Outdoor grill: 4 to 6 minutes; for best results, cut each ear of corn crosswise into 3 pieces before grilling

Note: Corn cannot be cooked on a contact grill unless the grill can be opened flat.

Warm Potato Salad, Midwest Style

Makes 6 servings

5 to 6 medium boiling potatoes
¼ cup cider vinegar
1 tablespoon sugar
2 teaspoons olive oil
1 medium red onion, sliced
Olive oil-flavored cooking spray
2 slices reduced-fat bacon
Salt and pepper to taste
2 tablespoons minced fresh parsley

Cover potatoes with salted water in a large pan. Bring to a boil, reduce heat to medium and cook 15 to 25 minutes, or until potatoes can be pierced easily with a fork, but are still firm. Cool. Peel potatoes and cut into ¼-inch-thick slices. (You can cook potatoes ahead of time and refrigerate, covered, for up to 2 days.)

In small bowl, combine vinegar, sugar, and oil. Set aside. Stir before using.

Preheat grill according to manufacturer's directions. Grill bacon for 2 to 4 minutes, turning as needed, or until browned and crisp. Remove to a paper towel. Don't clean grill. Place onion slices on grill and cook for 1 to 4 minutes, turning as needed, until lightly browned. Remove onion slices to a serving bowl.

Spray potato slices lightly with cooking spray. Grill for 2 to 5 minutes, turning as needed, until crispy on the outside and warm on the inside. Add to bowl with onions. Add vinegar dressing, salt and pepper, and parsley, and toss gently. Crumble the cooled bacon and sprinkle on top. Serve warm.

Outdoor grill: Cook bacon in a pan on the stovetop, not on grill (it will cause flareups); 6 to 8 minutes for potatoes, 4 to 6 minutes for onions

Italian-Style Potatoes and Carrots

Makes 6 servings

1 pound small, red new potatoes
3 large carrots, peeled and cut in half crosswise
2 tablespoons olive oil
1 teaspoon minced garlic
1 teaspoon dried oregano
1½ tablespoons minced fresh parsley
3 tomatoes, chopped
Salt and pepper to taste
Butter-flavored cooking spray

Cover potatoes and carrots with salted water in a large pan. Bring to a boil, reduce heat to medium and continue cooking for 10 to 20 minutes, or until potatoes and carrots are tender but still firm. Cool. Peel and slice potatoes ¼ inch thick. Slice carrots on the diagonal ¼ inch thick.

While potatoes are cooking, heat oil in a frying pan. Add garlic and cook for 1 minute over medium heat. Stir in oregano, parsley, and tomatoes. Season with salt and pepper to taste. Simmer for 5 to 6 minutes, stirring occasionally, until tomatoes soften. Remove from heat.

Preheat grill according to manufacturer's directions. Spray potato and carrot slices with cooking spray. Grill 2 to 5 minutes, turning as needed, or until potatoes and carrots are warmed through and crispy on the outside. Remove potatoes and carrots to serving bowl. Add tomato mixture, and toss. Serve hot.

Outdoor grill: 6 to 8 minutes

Moroccan-Style Pasta Salad

Makes 4 servings

1 small package (6 or 8 ounces) whole wheat pasta
2 tablespoons extra virgin olive oil
1½ cups plain nonfat yogurt
¾ teaspoon ground cumin
½ teaspoon salt
½ teaspoon minced garlic
1 fresh tomato, chopped
1 (15-ounce) can chick-peas (garbanzos), drained
2 bunches green onions, trimmed and chopped
3 red bell peppers, seeded, cut lengthwise into thirds
Olive oil-flavored cooking spray

Cook pasta according to package directions; drain.

While pasta is cooking, whisk together olive oil, yogurt, cumin, salt, and garlic. Set aside.

Place drained pasta in deep bowl. Toss with tomato, chick-peas, green onions, and yogurt dressing. Set aside.

Preheat grill according to manufacturer's directions. Spray peppers with cooking spray. Grill 3 to 5 minutes, turning as needed, or until peppers begin to char. Slice peppers into narrow strips. Add to pasta.

Divide salad onto serving dishes. Serve at room temperature or cold, with wedges of warm pita bread.

Outdoor grill: 7 to 10 minutes

Garlicky Eggplant and Olive Salad

Makes 6 servings

1 large eggplant, cut into ¼- to ½-inch slices
2 tablespoons salt
Garlic-flavored cooking spray
1 onion, sliced
1 large ripe tomato, chopped
½ cup pitted, chopped green olives
½ teaspoon ground cumin
1 teaspoon minced garlic
1 tablespoon extra virgin olive oil
Salt and pepper to taste

Sprinkle eggplant slices with salt. Let stand 20 minutes. Rinse off salt, and pat eggplant dry with paper toweling.

Preheat grill according to manufacturer's directions. Spray grilling surface with cooking spray. Spray eggplant slices with cooking spray. Grill about 5 to 8 minutes, turning as needed, or until crunchy and golden brown outside and soft on the inside. Set aside.

Spray onion slices and grill 2 to 4 minutes, turning as needed, until lightly browned and softened. Coarsely chop eggplant and onion and place in a serving bowl. Stir in tomato, olives, cumin, garlic, olive oil, and salt and pepper.

Serve warm or cold. If you refrigerate the salad, stir it before serving.

Outdoor grill: 15 to 20 minutes for eggplant, 8 to 10 minutes for onion

Leeks With Tomatoes and Basil

Makes 4 servings

3 tablespoons extra virgin olive oil
2 tablespoons minced fresh basil
1 teaspoon minced garlic
4 medium-sized leeks, trimmed, cut in half lengthwise,
   and washed well
Olive oil-flavored cooking spray
1 tablespoon freshly squeezed lemon juice
2 large ripe tomatoes, sliced
Salt and pepper to taste
Feta cheese (optional)

In a small bowl, mix together the oil, basil, and garlic. Set aside.

Spray cut leeks with cooking spray.

Preheat the grill according to manufacturer's directions. Spray grilling surface with cooking spray. Grill leeks over medium heat, cut side down, for 4 to 8 minutes, turning as needed, or until leeks are lightly charred and beginning to soften. Remove to a serving dish. Sprinkle with lemon juice.

Surround leeks with sliced tomatoes (if desired, you can grill tomatoes briefly to warm them). Drizzle basil-flavored oil over the leeks and tomatoes. Season with salt and pepper. If desired, sprinkle with a little feta cheese. Serve warm.

Outdoor grill: 10 to 12 minutes

Note: Leeks tend to be very sandy. Wash them thoroughly.

Portobello Mushrooms With Fresh Herbs

Makes 4 servings

4 large Portobello mushrooms, wiped clean with a
   damp paper towel, stems removed
¼ cup minced fresh mint
1 tablespoon minced fresh thyme
2 tablespoons minced fresh basil
2 tablespoons minced flat leaf parsley
¼ cup extra virgin olive oil
Olive oil-flavored cooking spray
Grated pecorino cheese or balsamic vinegar
Salt and pepper to taste

Remove mushroom stems and reserve for flavoring soups or stews. Wipe mushroom caps clean with a damp paper towel. Set aside. Mix mint, thyme, basil, and parsley with olive oil. Spread or dab herb mixture over both sides of mushrooms.

Preheat grill according to manufacturer's directions. Spray grilling surface with cooking spray. Cook mushrooms 8 to 14 minutes, turning as needed, or until they soften and turn dark brown. Do not overcook; you do not want them mushy. Season with salt and pepper. Serve hot, sprinkled with a little cheese or balsamic vinegar.

Outdoor grill: 10 to 15 minutes

Note: Portobello mushrooms are a very large, meaty, cultivated mushroom. They can be served as an appetizer, a vegetable side dish, between slices of bread as a vegetarian sandwich, or sliced into pasta or rice.

Grilled White and Brown Mushrooms

Makes 4 servings

½ pound brown Italian mushrooms
½ pound large white mushrooms
Olive oil-flavored cooking spray
Garlic powder, salt, and pepper to taste
1 teaspoon dried marjoram
Large, peeled garlic cloves (optional)
Toasted pine nuts (optional)

Clean mushrooms by wiping dirt off with a damp paper towel. Remove stems and reserve for another use (they're good for flavoring soups).

Spray mushrooms with cooking spray and sprinkle with garlic powder, salt, pepper, and marjoram.

Preheat grill according to manufacturer's directions. Spray grilling surface with cooking spray.

Cook mushrooms 4 to 8 minutes, turning as necessary, depending on thickness of mushrooms. Mushrooms should be soft but not mushy on the inside and golden on the outside.

If desired, spray garlic cloves with cooking spray and grill for 8 to 12 minutes, until golden and soft.

Remove mushrooms to a serving plate and sprinkle with grilled garlic and perhaps a few pine nuts if desired.

Outdoor grill: 6 to 8 minutes for mushrooms, 10 to 15 minutes for garlic

Note: You can substitute fresh shiitake and/or oyster mushrooms for some or all of the regular mushrooms. Oyster mushrooms will need to grill very briefly, 2 to 3 minutes.

Artichoke and Mushroom Kabobs

Makes 4 servings

½ freshly squeezed lemon or lime
¼ cup extra virgin olive oil
1 tablespoon dried basil
1 teaspoon minced garlic
2 bay leaves
1 (14½-ounce) can artichoke hearts, drained
12 medium mushrooms, cleaned and trimmed
4 bamboo skewers, soaked in water 10 minutes, drained

To make marinade: Combine juice, oil, basil, garlic, and bay leaves. Pour marinade into self-sealing plastic bag. Add artichokes and mushrooms. Seal bag securely closed. Turn bag several times so marinade coats all the vegetables. Refrigerate and marinate for 2 hours. Drain, discarding marinade.

Thread artichokes and mushrooms alternately onto skewers.

Preheat grill according to manufacturer's directions. Grill vegetable kabobs for 4 to 6 minutes, turning as needed, until tender and beginning to brown. Remove kabobs from the grill, set decoratively on the platter and serve on buffet or pass at the table. Serve hot or at room temperature.

Outdoor grill: 8 to 10 minutes

Grilled Fennel and Summer Squash

Makes 4 servings

2 bulbs fresh fennel, trimmed
2 medium-size yellow summer squash, trimmed
Olive oil-flavored cooking spray
1 tablespoon freshly squeezed lemon juice
1 tablespoon rice vinegar
2 tablespoons extra virgin olive oil
Salt and pepper to taste

Slice fennel lengthwise into ¼-inch slices, leaving core intact. Cut squash in half crosswise, then cut each half in half again lengthwise. Spray vegetables with cooking spray.

Preheat grill according to manufacturer's directions. Spray grilling surface with cooking spray. Cook fennel for 3 to 5 minutes, turning once, or until lightly browned but still fairly crisp. Grill squash, cut side down, for 3 to 5 minutes, until lightly browned and slightly softened. Remove fennel and squash to a serving dish. In a small bowl, whisk together lemon juice, vinegar, and olive oil. Drizzle over vegetables. Season with salt and pepper. Serve warm.

Outdoor grill: 6 to 8 minutes for fennel and squash

Zucchini Two Ways

Makes 4 servings

½ teaspoon minced garlic
¼ teaspoon salt
¼ teaspoon pepper
Olive oil-flavored cooking spray
3 small zucchini, about 4 inches long, cut into quarters
   lengthwise
½ cup chopped dry-roasted almonds
Cooked Tomato Sauce (Page 91)

Mix garlic, salt, and pepper and set aside while you prepare the zucchini. Preheat grill according to manufacturer's directions. Spray grilling surface with cooking spray. Spray zucchini with cooking spray and cook, cut side down, for about 3 to 4 minutes, turning as needed, or until lightly browned and tender but still crisp. Remove zucchini to serving plate. Sprinkle half the zucchini with almonds and spoon tomato sauce over the rest.

Outdoor grill: 6 to 8 minutes

Unfried Green Tomatoes

Makes 4 servings

¾ cup cornmeal
¼ teaspoon garlic powder
¼ teaspoon dried sage
¼ teaspoon salt
¼ teaspoon pepper
3 large green tomatoes, cut into ½-inch slices
Olive oil-flavored cooking spray
2 tablespoons minced parsley

Mix cornmeal with garlic powder, sage, salt, and pepper. Spread on a flat plate. Lightly dust both sides of green tomato slices with flavored cornmeal.

Preheat grill according to manufacturer's directions. Spray grilling surface with cooking spray. Cook tomato slices about 1 to 4 minutes, turning as needed, until crusty on the outside and warm on the inside.

Remove tomato slices to serving plate; sprinkle with parsley. Serve tomato slices hot.

Outdoor grill: 4 to 6 minutes

Note: Do not cook tomatoes on a contact grill unless it can be opened flat.

Parsnips and Pears

Makes 6 servings

6 medium parsnips, peeled, cut into quarters lengthwise
2 tablespoons dark brown sugar
⅛ teaspoon ground cinnamon
2 tablespoons margarine or butter, melted
4 firm, ripe pears, peeled, seeded, cut lengthwise into
    quarters
Butter-flavored cooking spray

Place parsnips in a saucepan and cover with water. Bring to a simmer and cook about 20 minutes, or until tender but still firm. Drain and cool.

Meanwhile, mix brown sugar, cinnamon, and margarine.

Preheat grill according to manufacturer's directions. Spray with cooking spray. Brush parsnips and pear pieces with the sugar mixture. Grill them, turning as needed, for 2 to 4 minutes, or until warm and tender. Remove to a serving dish. Serve hot.

Outdoor grill: 3 to 5 minutes

This is a lovely dish for fall, when sweet parsnips and pears are at their peak. Choose crisp, creamy-colored parsnips.

Acorn Squash With Brown Sugar

Makes 4 servings

2 acorn squash, cut in half, seeded
Butter-flavored cooking spray
¼ cup firmly packed dark brown sugar
¼ teaspoon salt
¼ teaspoon pepper
¼ teaspoon ground cinnamon
½ cup chopped walnuts

Cover acorn squash halves with cold water in a large saucepan. Bring to a boil over medium heat and continue cooking for 20 minutes or until the squash can be pierced easily with a fork, yet are still firm. Drain and cool.

Peel squash and cut into ½-inch rings. Spray with cooking spray. Mix brown sugar with salt, pepper, and cinnamon. Sprinkle over squash.

Preheat grill according to manufacturer's directions. Spray grilling surface with cooking spray. Grill squash rings over medium heat for 2 to 4 minutes, turning as needed. Squash will begin to brown on each side. Place squash on serving plate and sprinkle with walnuts. Serve hot.

Outdoor grill: 6 to 8 minutes

Plantains

Makes 4 to 6 servings

3 large, ripe plantains
Butter-flavored cooking spray
3 tablespoons minced cilantro, divided
Salt to taste

Peel plantains and cut into ½-inch slices. Press down on plantain slices with a spatula to flatten them slightly. Put plantain slices on a dish, set aside.

Spray plantains with cooking spray. Sprinkle with ½ tablespoon cilantro.

Preheat grill according to manufacturer's directions. Cook plantain slices for 2 to 4 minutes, or until golden brown on the outside and tender and warm on the inside.

Remove plantain slices to serving dish. Sprinkle with salt and remaining cilantro. Serve hot. Good as an appetizer or a vegetable course.

Outdoor grill: 6 to 8 minutes

Note: Although they look like bananas, plantains taste a bit like squash. They do not peel as easily as bananas. It's easiest to cut them in half, then use a small, sharp knife to slit the peel.

Sweet Potato Chips

Makes 4 servings

3 medium–large sweet potatoes
Butter-flavored cooking spray
½ teaspoon garlic powder
¼ teaspoon ground nutmeg
¼ teaspoon ground cinnamon
Salt to taste

Peel sweet potatoes. Cut in half. Cover potatoes with salted water in a large saucepan. Bring to a boil, reduce heat and cook over medium heat for 15 to 20 minutes or until potatoes can be pierced easily with a fork but are still firm. Drain and cool.

Slice sweet potatoes ¼ inch thick and set on a plate. Spray with cooking spray and sprinkle with garlic powder, nutmeg, and cinnamon.

Preheat grill according to manufacturer's directions. Spray grilling surface with cooking spray. Cook sweet potato slices for 2 to 4 minutes, turning as needed, or until potatoes are cooked and warm on the inside and crisp on the outside. Remove to serving dish; sprinkle with salt. Serve hot.

Outdoor grill: 6 to 8 minutes

Polenta With Fresh Tomato Salsa

Makes 6 servings

Olive oil-flavored cooking spray
4 cups water
2 teaspoons salt
1½ cups yellow cornmeal
2 tablespoons margarine or butter
Fresh Tomato Salsa (Page 92)

Spray a 9-by-5-inch or 8-by-4-inch loaf pan with cooking spray.

Bring water and salt to a boil over high heat. Add cornmeal in a slow steady stream, stirring constantly with a wooden spoon and pressing out lumps. Stir until all the cornmeal has been added. Simmer and stir continuously until mixture is thick and pulls away from sides of pan, about 20 to 25 minutes. Mix in margarine.

Pour polenta into prepared pan. Cool polenta, then refrigerate until firm, about 1 hour. Remove polenta from pan and cut into ½-inch slices.

Preheat grill according to manufacturer's directions. Spray grilling surface with cooking spray. Spray 6 polenta slices with cooking spray. Cook polenta for 2 to 5 minutes, turning as needed, until brown on the outside and warmed through. Serve polenta hot with tomato sauce.

Outdoor grill: 5 to 8 minutes

Note: Although homemade polenta tastes fresher, to save time you can grill ready-made packaged polenta, available in many supermarkets in the Italian foods aisle.

Polenta With Sage

Makes 4 servings

4 cups water
2 teaspoons salt
1½ cups yellow cornmeal
1 teaspoon dried sage, divided
2 tablespoons margarine, melted
Olive oil-flavored cooking spray

Spray a 9-by-5-inch or 8-by-4-inch loaf pan with cooking spray.

Bring water and salt to a boil over high heat. Add cornmeal in a slow steady stream, stirring constantly with a wooden spoon and pressing out lumps. Stir until all the cornmeal has been added. Simmer and stir continuously for about 20 to 25 minutes, or until mixture is thick and pulls away from sides of pan. Mix in ½ teaspoon sage and the margarine.

Pour polenta into prepared pan. Cool polenta, then refrigerate until firm, about 1 hour. Remove polenta from pan and cut into ½-inch slices. Spray polenta with cooking spray and sprinkle with ½ teaspoon sage.

Preheat grill according to manufacturer's directions. Spray grilling surface with cooking spray. Cook polenta for 2 to 5 minutes, turning as needed, or until polenta is just browned on the outside and warmed through. Serve hot.

Outdoor grill: 5 to 8 minutes

Tofu and Slaw Sandwich

Makes 4 servings

1 pound firm tofu

Nonfat cooking spray

¾ cup Tangy Barbecue Sauce (Page 95), or your favorite bottled barbecue sauce

4 cups shredded green cabbage (or cabbage-carrot mix)

¼ cup rice vinegar

2 tablespoons sugar

¼ teaspoon salt

1 tablespoon light mayonnaise

4 hamburger rolls, split

Drain and rinse tofu. Cut crosswise into 8 slices. Place tofu slices between paper towels and gently but firmly press tofu to squeeze out moisture. Spray a shallow glass dish or plate with cooking spray and place tofu in dish. Spoon barbecue sauce over tofu and turn to coat tofu on all sides. Cover and refrigerate for several hours or overnight.

While tofu marinates, make slaw. Combine cabbage with rice vinegar, sugar, salt, and mayonnaise. Refrigerate until serving time.

Preheat grill according to manufacturer's directions. Place rolls, cut side down, on the grill to lightly toast them. (Do not toast on a closed contact grill.) Set aside.

Spray the grill surface with cooking spray. Grill tofu 3 to 7 minutes, turning as needed, until nicely browned and crisp.

Place tofu on rolls and top with a spoonful or two of the slaw. Replace tops of rolls. Serve sandwiches immediately, with any remaining slaw on the side.

Outdoor grill: 6 to 8 minutes

Bruschetta

Makes 4 servings

4 large slices day-old Italian or French bread, cut ½
   inch thick
Olive oil-flavored cooking spray
2 medium cloves garlic, peeled and cut in half
Extra virgin olive oil
1 large tomato, chopped
1 small red onion, minced

Preheat grill according to manufacturer's directions. Spray grilling surface with cooking spray. Grill bread for 30 seconds to 3 minutes, turning as needed, until toasted. Watch it closely so it does not burn.

Remove bread from grill and set on a serving platter. Lightly rub top side of bread with cut sides of garlic cloves; discard garlic. Drizzle bread with olive oil, then sprinkle with chopped tomato and minced red onion.

Serve hot.

Outdoor grill: 2 to 3 minutes; do not put directly over coals or flame

Note: Bruschetta, a simple Italian classic, is the original inspiration for garlic bread. It always is flavored with garlic and good oil, but the other toppings vary according to the region and the cook.

Grilled Fruit Salad With Ginger Chutney Dressing

Makes 6 servings

¾ cup bottled mango chutney, or Papaya or Mango
  Chutney (Page 94)
¼ cup chopped candied ginger (available in spice area
  of most supermarkets)
1 cup plain nonfat yogurt
2 heads Bibb lettuce, separated (or a 6- to 8-ounce bag
  salad mix)
1 cantaloupe, peeled, seeded, cut into 1-inch wedges
1 peeled, cored, and sliced pineapple, drained
2 bananas, peeled, sliced lengthwise
Butter-flavored cooking spray

Combine chutney, ginger, and yogurt. Cover and refrigerate until needed. Stir before serving.

Arrange lettuce on plates.

Preheat grill according to manufacturer's directions. Spray grilling surface with cooking spray. Spray fruits with cooking spray. Grill cantaloupe wedges and pineapple slices about 1 to 3 minutes, turning as needed, until lightly golden. Arrange on salad plates. Grill bananas 1 to 2 minutes, turning as needed, until lightly golden. Arrange fruits on top of lettuce.

Drizzle chutney dressing over fruit and serve immediately.

Outdoor grill: 2 to 4 minutes for all the fruit

Grilled Pound Cake With Raspberry Sauce

Makes 6 servings

1 (10-ounce) package frozen raspberries, defrosted,
  juice included
2 teaspoons freshly squeezed lime juice
¼ cup sugar
Butter-flavored cooking spray
3 1-inch-thick slices reduced-fat pound cake

Reserve a few raspberries for garnish. Puree remaining raspberries in a blender or a food processor fitted with the steel blade. Combine lime juice and sugar with raspberries in a small saucepan. Simmer for 3 to 4 minutes. Strain sauce, discarding seeds. Set aside.

Preheat grill according to manufacturer's directions. Spray grilling surface with cooking spray. Spray cake slices with cooking spray. Grill 1 to 2 minutes, turning as needed, or just until warmed through and lightly toasted.

Spoon raspberry sauce into individual dishes. Set a slice of cake on each plate over the sauce. Sprinkle with reserved raspberries. Serve immediately.

Outdoor grill: 1 to 2 minutes

Note: This is also good with angel food, which must be cooked on an open grill (not a closed contact grill). You can substitute sliced, lightly sweetened peaches for the raspberry sauce.

Orange Slices With Blueberries

Makes 6 servings

4 large navel oranges, peeled, cut into ¼-inch slices
1 cup dry sherry, divided
1 pint blueberries
2 tablespoons dry sherry
3 tablespoons light brown sugar
2 tablespoons margarine or butter
Butter-flavored cooking spray

Place orange slices in a bowl. Remove 2 tablespoons sherry and set aside. Pour remaining sherry over the oranges. Let stand at room temperature for 1 hour, turning once. Drain.

Meanwhile pick over blueberries, discarding any bruised berries. Wash berries and drain on paper towels. Place berries in a bowl and toss with 2 tablespoons sherry. Set aside.

Preheat grill according to manufacturer's directions. Mix brown sugar and margarine together. Sprinkle on oranges. Spray grilling surface with cooking spray. Grill orange slices for 1 to 3 minutes, turning as necessary, or until warmed through and golden. Set warm orange slices on dessert plates. Sprinkle with blueberries and serve immediately.

Outdoor grill: 2 to 4 minutes

Papaya or Honeydew With Strawberries

Makes 4 servings

1 cup nonfat vanilla yogurt
2 tablespoons firmly packed light brown sugar
1 tablespoon dark rum, or 1 teaspoon vanilla extract
1 large papaya or 1 small honeydew melon (enough for 4 servings)
Butter-flavored cooking spray
1 pint fresh strawberries, washed, stemmed, and sliced

Mix yogurt, sugar, and rum together. Spoon into a bowl. Refrigerate until serving time.

Peel, seed, and cut the papaya into ¾-inch-wide spears. If using honeydew, peel, seed, and cut into thin wedges. Spray with cooking spray. Preheat grill according to manufacturer's directions. Spray grilling surface with cooking spray. Cook papaya or melon 1 to 3 minutes, turning as needed, or until lightly golden and warmed through. Remove to serving dish. Serve immediately, topped with strawberries and drizzled with vanilla yogurt mixture.

Outdoor grill: 2 to 4 minutes

Grilled Bananas

Makes 4 servings

2 tablespoons margarine or butter, melted
2 tablespoons light brown sugar
¼ teaspoon ground cinnamon
⅛ teaspoon ground nutmeg
4 large ripe but firm bananas, cut in half lengthwise
Butter-flavored cooking spray

Mix margarine with brown sugar, cinnamon, and nutmeg. Brush bananas with sugar mixture.

Preheat grill according to manufacturer's directions. Spray grilling surface with cooking spray. Cook bananas for 1 to 2 minutes, turning as needed, or until they are beginning to turn golden. Serve warm, plain or with a scoop of low-fat vanilla ice cream or frozen yogurt.

Outdoor grill: 2 to 4 minutes

Sauces, Marinades, Seasonings

Condiments are key to great grilling. Who could imagine a hot dog without mustard, a burrito without salsa, or bruschetta without extra virgin olive oil?

The average supermarket these days carries an impressive array of vinegars, the basic ingredient in most marinades and dressings. Try them all, plain or seasoned with herbs or spices, in marinades and quick salad dressings: sherry, red wine, cider, rice vinegar, white wine, tarragon, regular and white balsamic vinegars.

Sprinkling a bit of herb or spice into the marinade or over the food before grilling can also do wonders. At the least, stock your cupboard with such basics as garlic powder, rosemary, thyme, tarragon, basil, red pepper, cinnamon, and chili powder. Basil, dill, cilantro, and parsley taste better fresh, but can be used dried in marinades and dressings.

Lean foods often benefit from a bath in marinade, a seasoned liquid that's used to tenderize, moisten, and flavor foods. Marinades always contain an acid of some sort to tenderize the food and help flavors penetrate. A bit of oil in a marinade helps moisten food and keep it from sticking to the grill surface. To add a smidgen of oil quickly, spray the food on both sides with cooking spray before putting it in the bag with the other marinade ingredients.

Foods should be marinated in non-metal containers. Gallon-size, self-sealing plastic freezer bags are especially convenient. Place the marinade ingredients in the bag, zip it shut, and shake to mix up the ingredients (do this over the sink to be on the safe side). Open the bag and slide in the food, then zip it shut again. Just in case of leaks, place the bag in a bowl. Even though marinades contain acids, marinating foods do need to be refrigerated.

Many foods can sit in a marinade for several hours, though no food should marinate for longer than 24 hours; it will turn mushy. Fish, especially, should be marinated for a relatively short time; the acid in the marinade can begin to "cook" and toughen the fish.

This chapter also has recipes for sauces that go wonderfully with grilled foods. The fresh tomato salsa can be used on everything from fish to beef fajitas. Cooked tomato sauce is wonderful on grilled eggplant or summer squash, as well as meats and, of course, pasta. Try the papaya chutney with poultry or pork. The tangy barbecue sauce is good on all kinds of meat and poultry, as well as tofu and vegetables.

Cooked Tomato Sauce

Makes about 5 cups; enough for 4 to 6 servings

Olive oil-flavored cooking spray
1 clove garlic, minced
1 onion, minced
½ pound ground beef
1 (28-ounce) can tomatoes, undrained
1 (6-ounce) can tomato paste
¾ cup water
2 bay leaves
¾ teaspoon dried basil
½ teaspoon dried oregano
Salt and pepper to taste

Spray frying pan generously with cooking spray and heat over medium heat. Cook garlic and onion for 4 minutes, stirring occasionally. Mix in ground beef and cook about 10 minutes, breaking the meat into small pieces with a spatula or spoon, until the meat is just browned. Add tomatoes and juice, tomato paste, water, bay leaves, basil, oregano, salt and pepper. Simmer, partially covered, about 45 minutes, or until sauce thickens. Stir occasionally during cooking and use spoon to break up tomato chunks. Add more water if needed. Discard bay leaves. To serve, place grilled vegetables or meat on serving dish and cover with tomato sauce. Serve hot.

Fresh Tomato Salsa

Makes about 1½ cups; enough for 4 servings

3 medium, ripe tomatoes, chopped
⅓ cup finely chopped red onion
3 to 4 tablespoons finely chopped fresh cilantro, to taste
1 to 2 jalapeno peppers, finely chopped, to taste
Salt to taste

Combine all ingredients in a glass bowl. Refrigerate. Stir just before serving.

Note: For a Mediterranean-style sauce, omit the jalapeno pepper and cilantro and add 1 to 2 tablespoons of chopped fresh basil, thyme, or rosemary.

Basic Marinade

Makes about 1 cup, enough to marinate 1 to 1½ pounds of food

¾ cup vinegar, dry wine, or citrus juice
¼ cup extra virgin olive oil
1 teaspoon minced garlic (optional)
¼ cup chopped fresh herbs, or 2 to 3 teaspoons dried
  herbs
2 bay leaves

Combine all ingredients in a large, self-sealing plastic freezer bag. Add meat or other food to be marinated. Seal bag shut, turning bag to coat food with marinade. Place in a bowl in the refrigerator.

Marinate chicken for 1 to 4 hours, meat for 2 hours to overnight, fish or shellfish for 1 to 2 hours, and vegetables for 1 to 2 hours.

Notes: Use red wine or red wine vinegar for beef, lamb, and dark-meat poultry. Use white wine vinegar or lemon or lime juice for white-meat poultry, pork, fish, and vegetables. Orange juice tastes good with just about any kind of food.

Try basil, mint, cilantro, marjoram, dill, tarragon, or rosemary with milder flavored foods such as chicken or turkey, fish, pork, and most vegetables. Thyme, rosemary, mustard, and pepper go nicely with pork, lamb, beef, dark-meat poultry, and full-flavored fish such as salmon. Sage and oregano go with either light or dark meats. Parsley is an "all-purpose" herb that goes with just about anything.

Papaya or Mango Chutney

Makes about 2 cups

1 pound papaya or mango cubes (about 2 cups)
½ cup white vinegar
¾ cup sugar
1 small onion, chopped
1 teaspoon minced ginger
½ cup golden raisins
½ teaspoon minced garlic
½ teaspoon crushed red pepper
1 teaspoon ground cinnamon
½ teaspoon ground cloves

Combine all ingredients in a large, stainless steel saucepan. Bring to a boil, then reduce heat to medium. Continue cooking until papaya is tender. Reduce heat to a simmer and cook, stirring occasionally, until chutney is thick, about 10 minutes longer. Let cool. Taste and adjust seasonings as necessary. Spoon into clean glass jars and refrigerate until needed. Stir before serving.

Note: Homemade chutney can be bottled to make a nice gift. Pour it into 2 sterile half-pint jars, seal, and process in a boiling water bath for 10 minutes. Or, simply keep refrigerated and instruct the recipient to do the same.

Tangy Barbecue Sauce

Makes about 1¼ cups; enough for about 6 servings

¾ cup ketchup
¼ cup molasses
2 tablespoons brown sugar
¼ cup cider vinegar
1 tablespoon Worcestershire sauce
Hot red pepper sauce, to taste
Salt and pepper to taste

Combine all ingredients in a non–aluminum saucepan. Bring to a simmer, then turn heat to low and simmer for 10 minutes, stirring frequently. Remove from heat and let cool. Refrigerate. If poured into a clean jar and kept refrigerated, this sauce will keep for up to 2 weeks.

Note: Because of the sugar content, this (and similar barbecue sauces) can burn easily. Brush it lightly on foods before grilling, and turn the food at least once, even if you're using a contact grill. Reheat remaining sauce and brush or spoon a little over the grilled food just before serving.

Index

About the author

Barbara Grunes is the best-selling author of more than 40 cookbooks, including *Fish on the Grill, Shellfish on the Grill, Poultry on the Grill, The Beef Lover's Great Grill Book,* and *The Complete Idiot's Guide to Grilling.* She lives near Chicago with her husband, Jerry.

Look for more cookbooks at our Web sites, snowcappress.com and cookbookauthors.com.

We carry our own cookbooks, as well as selected, hard-to-find cookbooks written for other publishers, often at significant discounts from the original cover prices.

We now sell electronic cookbooks as well as print books, including an e-book version of *Healthy Grilling*.